THIS SIGNED EDITION OF

# Your Money OR Your Life

BY

## NEIL CAVUTO

HAS BEEN SPECIALLY BOUND BY THE PUBLISHER

# Your Money or Your Life

**Also by Neil Cavuto**

*More Than Money*

# Your Money OR Your Life

# NEIL CAVUTO

ReganBooks
*An Imprint of* HarperCollins*Publishers*

HarperCollins books may be purchased for educational, business, or sales promotional use. For information please write: Special Markets Department, HarperCollins Publishers Inc., 10 East 53rd Street, New York, NY 10022.

FIRST EDITION

*Designed by Publications Development Company of Texas*

Printed on acid-free paper

Library of Congress Cataloging-in-Publication Data has been applied for.

ISBN-10: 0-06-082617–7

ISBN-13: 978-0-06-082617-8

05 06 07 08 09 PDC/RRD 10 9 8 7 6 5 4 3 2 1

To Mom and Dad,
Kathleen and Patrick Cavuto.
You've left this world, but to this day you
remain the guiding force in my world.

# CONTENTS

# *INTRODUCTION*

Some time back a friend of mine wanted to know how it was possible that I had the number one–rated daily business show on cable television. "I think I know," he said. "It's because you're so weird."

He meant that in jest. But it resonated with me, because I think he was right. I am weird, and my show is weirder still. I don't have a problem with weird. I like weird. I like weird chief executives, weird politicians, and weird moments in life. I think weirdness defines us, and that the best among us often are a little more unusual than the rest of us.

That's why I try not to distinguish between business news and general news. To me, the two are the same. Why distinguish and compartmentalize as if one side of the brain goes in one editorial direction and the other side in another direction? I don't. I don't think most people do, either. Just think of how business journalists limit themselves when they see the world through a business-only prism. They almost invite the rest of the world to tune out.

It's why I say, without a moment's hesitation, that I value ratings. I really value the fact that a lot of folks watch me—not just rich folks, or investing folks, but everyday folks, with everyday concerns. That means I'm talking to regular folks, not preaching to them. Over the quarter century I've been doing this—first in print, then in broadcasting, then in print *and* broadcasting—I'm amazed at how many people seem to believe that if it's about Wall Street, it's not about Main Street. I think it's the other way around. Wall Street *is* Main Street. It's why I don't distinguish between them, and it's why I don't forget on which side my bread is buttered. The folks holding that butter knife aren't who you think they are. They're who we are.

I'm not saying I single-handedly democratized business news, but I think I have helped make it more mainstream. And trust me, that's not because I'm a genius, but precisely because I'm not. I always tell people I was never the smartest kid in my class, but I knew the right questions to ask. I work by an old rule of thumb a dear editor friend of mine from years back hammered into my head: "If you can't explain it to your mom, don't waste your time telling it to America." My boss and the chairman and chief executive of Fox News Channel, Roger Ailes, had another take: "When you've lost your audience, you've lost your show."

He was right then. He's right now, because about now people are hungering for context and meaning in the money they make, the place they make it, and ultimately the places they spend it. That's what my show is about each weekday, and what our powerful bloc of business programs on Fox are about on weekends.

Not only do we dare touch on issues others avoid, we find fascinating angles on issues others miss. I often tell viewers this is where "the spreadsheet hits the fan." I want to give viewers more—more meaning, more hope, and more depth. It's why, soon after 9/11, I focused not on the obvious loss of financial capital that day, but the very real, still undefined loss of human capital our economy suffered on that day.

Real people don't constantly spout statistics. Why should I? It's why I try to keep such nonsense to a minimum. I'll admit it's not always easy, but it's always my goal.

That's why I do something special in my show: I editorialize. Only at the end, and only over an issue that matters that day, that moves me that day, and that I trust will move others as well. Sometimes they're big issues, such as 9/11. Sometimes they're issues that don't seem very big at all, such as the plight of a harried cashier at Christmastime who gives her all to her customers, or a snippy receptionist who does not.

When I started doing these little comments at the end of my show, way back in my days at CNBC, they got curious reactions. Some viewers thought them novel, others reprehensible. But the reaction grew. And, as the availability of e-mail grew, so did the sheer number of responses. Today I get thousands of e-mails each day on issues that are hot, and even on some that are decidedly not. Viewers don't seem to discriminate. They relish the tidbits on the retired CEO who misses the good life, or the friendly doorman just trying to provide good service. Some cry. Some laugh. Still others scream. But rarely is the response lukewarm. They say in television that you want to generate heat. I want to generate *thought*, and do it with heat. There is a difference. One assumes that you merely entertain; the other appreciates the fact that you can inform and entertain.

To me, these reactions prove that certain issues resonate. I don't need people to agree with me—just to come along and think with me. Whether it's about being rich or dying young, about the powerful guy who lost it all or the little investor who won it all, I think I just try to strike a chord, for good or ill (which is why I also feature blistering and complimentary e-mails alike on the prior day's comments). I want to engage viewers. Let the debate begin. Let the thinking continue. One friendly viewer expressed concern that allowing damning e-mails from "crazies" on the show wasn't the stuff of highbrow anchordom. I agreed then; I agree now. But I didn't care then, and I don't care now. Look, with my slightly chunky, big-headed appearance, I don't seem like someone who stepped out of anchor central casting. So why should I act like I did? It'd be an act, and viewers would see through it quicker than I make my way through a Ponderosa dessert bar!

I am weird. But as I wrote in my last book, *More Than Money*, that's the way I am. Because I've survived cancer and am currently battling multiple sclerosis, I've learned to be philosophical about life's gives and takes. I don't say that to win your sympathy, but to give you an understanding of my thinking. Illnesses can whack you out, but they needn't freak you out. Sometimes they can force you to think, not about the life you have, but the life that you might not have . . . so that you appreciate the little things, the unusual things, and yes, the weird things.

Those are the things I notice. And those are the things I highlight in this book—a look back at nearly a decade's worth of reflection on everything from Bill Clinton's scandals to his successor's war. In its pages I cover the gamut, of careers made and careers lost, of fortunes scored and fortunes gone. I look back and remember the things I was lucky enough to get right—like warning about something called an Internet bubble—to the things I got wrong, like AOL and Time Warner coming together in a "stunning" merger that was bound for greatness.

I disliked the people others liked, including Alan Greenspan, and liked the people others disliked, including Al Dunlap. I was late to some parties, early to others, but I put it all out there, warts and all, and let the world know that day how I felt.

These are quick snapshots on days where the image paled almost as soon as the shutter was released. Some issues made me mad, others made me cry, still others made me howl, but all made me think. It's up to you now to decide whether, in the end, any of these made a difference. I hope, gamely, that they did, and that now, for you, they do.

# CHAPTER 1

# *YOUR MONEY, BUT NOT YOUR WHOLE LIFE*

*O*ne of the issues I wrestle with every day in my profession is money versus life. What does money matter if you're sick, or even worse, dead? What does all the wealth in the world matter if you have no one with whom to share it? One of my biggest challenges in doing my job is figuring out how to handle the show on those days when something horrible has happened before my hour. It could be a plane crash, terrorist act, a kidnapping—you name it.

Suddenly, in those moments, a show that talks about money seems to matter less, and the potential for appearing callous and indifferent bothers me more. That's why I argue to my bosses at Fox that mine is the toughest job at Fox—keeping loyal news viewers loyal to a business product as well. It's a tough juggling act, but I try to keep it simple. For me, it's not about the money, Stupid. It's about life, Stupid. Everything's intertwined. Everything's connected: Our lives. Our money. Our . . . everything.

That's why I always remind my staff that we should never forget the value of life, first, and doing something with it, second. It's why I like to put things in perspective. I've never hidden the *fact that I've dealt with illness in my life—first cancer, now multiple sclerosis. I'm no stranger to the ravages of illness; many in my family succumbed years ahead of their time.*

*Sadly, such things have shaped me and made me—as a man and as a journalist. They're why I can be such a sentimental moosh. I am moved easily. I cry even more easily. Such are not the qualities you'd expect in a tough, seasoned journalist, but I argue to the contrary. They have helped make me a better journalist, more willing to think outside the box—perhaps because I know that, in the end, we'll all end up in a box.*

*That sounds strange, I know, and I don't mean to come off as grim or glum—just as a guy who sees life as a fleeting, wonderful opportunity, to be savored and enjoyed. But most important, to be put in perspective. It's why some in my business have called me the antibusiness reporter. They're partly right. I'm not just about numbers and figures. I'm not married to earnings and acronyms. I am married to life and to everyday lessons—things that don't change like profit reports but from which we can all profit immensely.*

*Nowhere and at no time in my career have these two issues—money and life—collided as they did on September 11, 2001. The sheer enormity of the disaster defined generations and seared our conscience in a way that few events ever had. Ostensibly my job as a business reporter was to give the financial take on this disaster. Clearly, the site of the New York attack—but a stone's throw from the center of capitalism itself—was no accident. The World Trade Center embodied that capitalism; indeed, it housed many of its most prominent players.*

*But I couldn't look at this as just a financial event. I had interviewed too many of the very people who died that day, some of whom had been on my show just days earlier. No, this was more than simply a loss of financial capital. This was an enormous loss of human capital. I wanted that to be the story, and my message was to tell that story, again and again—the cruelty of it, the barbarity of it, the senselessness of it. I was sure then we would recover from that tragic day, but I wanted to remind all that this was about good and evil that day.*

*Some say it's not a business journalist's job to blather on about such issues. I disagreed then. I disagree now. After all, from my days back at CNBC more than a decade ago, I had no problem putting my emotion into my work then. I have had no problem putting my heart into the stories, particularly tragic stories like 9/11, since. One could argue that anchors must be passive, even emotionless, observers. By that definition, I guess I do not measure up. But in covering this story, from its sad first moments, to the legions of funerals and eulogies and tragic anniversaries that would follow, I'd cover it somewhat differently—not as a television anchor, but as something more: a human being.*

## After the Terror—Searching, Hoping

*September 18, 2001*

Finally, this hour, a small perspective on a huge event. A few little things that may help make sense of this big national pain.

So many of you have shared so many wonderful stories that speak volumes on the American spirit. Like Sally Anne Novak from Greensburg, Pennsylvania, who tells me of taking her mom out to lunch just to, as she says, "Get away from the television for a while." She mentioned the two policemen eating lunch behind her at the restaurant, and the stranger who quietly picked up their bill.

There's the trader on Wall Street who attached a picture of his buddy, feared dead, on his lapel. "I'm here for him," he says, "even though I'm not really here at all."

And those kids with the lemonade stand, raising hundreds of dollars for the relief effort, nickels and dimes and quarters at a time.

And the grade school students in New York who decided to draw flags and hand them out because there were no real flags to be found.

I know. Small stuff. But, I think, big stuff. Important stuff.

More important than stocks or money or investments or price earnings or EBIDTA, or any of that stuff.

A lot of my usual business guests talked about that stuff. A lot of them are gone.

Like David Alger of Alger Management, as warm and funny as he was prescient and just plain smart. A guy who once said of this market, "Neil, it's like life. Better things come along."

Or Bill Meehan of Cantor Fitzgerald, always offering me health advice with a smile and a wink, and one time inquiring about my favorite chocolate snack, "What exactly are Yodels?"

And the many others I talked to, listened to, and learned from. It's as if they were just here. Then, like that, they were not. One of life's cruel little twists that leaves a big, gaping void. And me, still wondering what it all means.

I have no idea.

# 9/11 and My Dad

### *September 24, 2001*

I'll never forget one of the saddest days of my life. It was my father's funeral.

A lot of important people were there—the heads of a lot of companies, including his own, and some politicians.

They impressed me, both by coming and by saying so many nice things about my dad. But I'll never forget the other folks who came. Truck drivers and restaurant owners who knew my dad well, and just wanted to pay their respects.

Some literally came right from work, hardly dressed for a wake or funeral, but hardly caring. Certainly I didn't.

They were the salt of the earth, the most decent folks you'd ever want to meet. Some gathered to say nice words. Others to say nothing at all. They said they'd set up a memorial. And they did. They meant what they said, they said what they meant. Little guys who stand for big things.

Just like little investors who we're now told did in fact buy stocks last week, while those big important guys sat on their hands. The folks at market research firm Biryini Associates confirming what I already knew . . . that small trades under ten thousand shares were positive last week right after the attacks. Trades over ten thousand shares were negative— actually, very negative.

Let me say that again: Small investors were buying. Big investors were selling.

Small investors bought what they could. Big investors sold pretty much anything they could.

Both aimed to show their patriotism.

I'm not saying it's un-American to sell. But it is un-American to say you won't, and then you do.

Some big guys did that.

No small guy that I know of even considered that.

Proof that the little guy has a big heart and doesn't make light of something called . . . his word.

# Forgive, but Don't Forget

*October 15, 2001*

What I'm about to say sounds like financial heresy. But here goes.

A lot of companies are going to come up with a lot of excuses for a lot of lousy sales and earnings numbers these next few weeks. I say we cut 'em slack. And let 'em.

I know more than a few of them are going to use the September 11 "event," as they're calling it, as a reason for all these troubles. Some are justified. Some are not.

I just don't think at this time we question them. Not now.

If some of those companies want to throw in the baby with the bath water, so be it. They can't do it forever, so let's let them do it now. Here's why.

There'll be plenty of time to scrutinize and attack. Now is not that time.

There'll be plenty of time to truly hold management accountable. Now is not that time.

There'll be plenty of time to see if all these layoffs were justified. Now is not that time.

So I say, give 'em a pass on this quarter. A lot of us do the same for our kids. Some are acting a bit strangely—maybe not doing as well at school, maybe more frustrated at home.

A lot is going on in their little lives. Who are we to play the heavy in their lives when they're dealing with all this heavy stuff?

So I want to treat companies just like we do our kids, with a bit more leeway and a lot more understanding.

I'd much rather hold them accountable for what they can do now, than for what they didn't do then.

Like our kids, they might be making excuses.
But like our kids, for now I'm gonna let 'em.

## Two Months After the Terror, the Crash of American Airlines Flight 587

*November 12, 2001*

Sometimes statistics don't really mean much. That's crazy for me, a business news guy, to say. But on a day like today, they mean even less. I know you're a thousand times more at risk in a car than on a plane. More likely to get hit crossing the street than flying above the street. Precisely because they are so rare, plane crashes garner so much attention. Especially now. Especially with a nation in fear.

I'm not here to judge what brought down American Airlines Flight 587 . . . though all signs, at least early on, point to some sort of mechanical failure. For the flying public, I don't think it matters. They're plain scared . . . of planes. But you can bet your bottom dollar it very much matters to the people who run our airline industry. Just as they were enticing people back into their planes, another reason for people to avoid them.

Had this happened prior to September 11, it might have given people pause. But it likely would not have given people panic. Now, many say they won't fly. I think that's a mistake, but a natural reaction.

Rallying the public's opinion is one thing. Overcoming their fears is quite another. They'll fight the good fight, but today that fight has become a lot tougher.

# Don't Let Evil Win

*October 12, 2001*

Fear is a powerful emotion. It can stop you. It can paralyze you. It can turn you inward. It can turn you away. From shopping malls. From movie theaters. From restaurants. And sporting events. It can take a sunny disposition and make it miserable. It can take hope and turn it into despair. It is a cancer that eats at our very soul. And inflicts all souls.

It is the stuff of which depressions are made, on a mind and on an economy. It stops people from buying stocks. It stops people from buying socks. It stops people, period.

And terrorists know it. They delight in it. They relish it. They look forward to it. And when they kill our people, they plan on it.

I say, enough of it. If for no other reason than because it gives them something to gloat over.

We are stronger than they are cruel. We are more hopeful than they are awful. We are as good as they are evil. They hope that by startling us, they can stop us, or at least slow us.

I say, they don't know us. The greatness of a people is defined not by the good times they enjoy, but by the tough times they endure. A good stock will always come back. Fundamentals dictate that. A good people will always come back. History proves that. The short seller will try to stop the good stock. But fail. Murderers will try to stop the good people. But will also fail. Miserably.

# Response to an Ass

*October 3, 2001*

(Responding to an e-mail from one Mr. Abraham, who condemned me for characterizing the September 11 attacks as "acts of terror." He argued that they were acts of war against a country that had victimized an oppressed people. For good measure, Mr. Abraham called me clueless and fat.)

Fat? I much prefer *hefty*. But to your bigger point, Mr. Abraham, you're an ass. And here's why.

If these attacks were military actions, then I'm Jack LaLanne. I'm not, and they're not. Killing innocent people whose greatest sin was showing up for work isn't justice. It's cowardice. Storming planes doesn't make you Patton. It does make you pathetic. And spouting your cause by ramming those planes into buildings doesn't make you awe-inspiring. Just awful.

This is not the time to try to explain evil, but to combat it. Not to justify attacks. But to counter those attacks. Save the hand wringing and psycho babbling about what this country did and didn't do for someone with a sympathetic ear.

I'm not that guy, Mr. Abraham.

You call me brainless and ignorant. Well, I'm smart enough to know this: The thousands who died three weeks ago weren't soldiers. They weren't terrorists. They were just average Joes and Joannes unlucky enough to be in the wrong place at the wrong time. They did nothing wrong. America has made its mistakes. But for the life of me, I can't ever recall our dancing in the streets after killing a bunch of innocent people.

I'm a business guy. So I see things as pretty black and white. And this much is clear. There's nothing heroic about being evil. Sometimes it's like a lousy stock. You know it . . . just looking at it.

## Why Not Call Terrorists What They Are?

*October 1, 2001*

There's something almost as ridiculous as not letting your employees wear American flag pins if they wish. How about not calling terrorists what they are—terrorists?

In case you haven't heard, a couple of news organizations, including one of those other news channels, are refusing to use the "T" word to describe those guys who hijacked planes three weeks ago and changed life as we know it here. They're now "suspected hijackers." That's like calling me "allegedly hefty." Please.

What's happening to my profession? Are we that stupid? Let's be clear. When you seize a plane and start killing passengers, you're a terrorist. When you take that same plane and ram it into a tower at the World Trade Center, you're a terrorist. When you do the exact same thing on another plane and ram it into the other tower of the World Trade Center, you're a terrorist. When you take over another plane and crash it into the Pentagon, you're a terrorist. When you take still another plane and try to go God knows where, unleashing God knows what agony on innocent passengers and those below, you're a terrorist. When you rip children from parents, you're a terrorist. When you rip from this life people whose only crime was trying to make something of this life, you're a terrorist.

The thousands who were disintegrated and obliterated three weeks ago are not "alleged victims." They're victims. And they're dead. All dead. They are mothers and fathers, brothers and sisters, friends and colleagues. All gone.

Suspected hijackers didn't do that. Terrorists did.

## Where Were You on September 10, 2001?

*September 10, 2002*

Where were you last September 10? A year ago today. Our nation's last day of innocence.

*USA Today*'s Rick Hampson offers a poignant, if not tearful, look back at the randomness of fate and the lives full of unexpected ironies.

There's the story of Joe Kelly, enjoying a rain-delayed Yankee game this night, a year ago, with his sons Christopher and Thomas. This will be his last full day on earth. The next day he's due early at work at the 105th floor of the North Tower.

September 10 is the first day on the job for Scott Vasel, an insurance disaster specialist of all things, who loved the view from his desk on the 97th floor of the North Tower.

There's Paul Beatini, who is staying home with his two little girls this day because his wife has a meeting. On September 11, he'll be at a meeting himself, on the 105th floor.

Or of Dorothy Chiarchiaro, who's a waitress at Windows on the World, the restaurant atop the North Tower. She normally works Mondays, but needs the day off to be with her granddaughters. She'll go in Tuesday, September 11, instead.

All gone now. All so vibrant and alive then.

There are snippets of a day that seems so far away. Construction at Newark Airport, causing delays. A big primary eve race in New York, causing some heated headlines. A World Trade Center developer who promises the sky's the limit for retailing there.

That night, it rains hard. The Yankees game is canceled. Joe Kelly takes his sleepy sons, Christopher and Thomas, back home. Early the next morning he leaves for work, before any of them are up. He never returns. The rest . . . is history.

Reminders, as if we need them, to treasure the moments. Because the moments . . . might not last.

## Something to Be Proud of Post-9/11

*September 2, 2002*

I'm always amazed by the resilience of the American spirit. I mean, put yourself back in time, a year ago Labor Day weekend. If you knew then that we'd be days away from a vicious terrorist attack on American soil that would claim nearly three thousand lives. . . . That shortly thereafter we would be conducting a war on terror unlike anything seen in American history. . . . That shortly after that, a company called Enron would implode, and soon scores of crooked corporate books would be brought to light. . . . That we'd have CEOs being herded off in handcuffs, executives pleading the Fifth on Capitol Hill, and shareholder lawsuits being filed by the dozens, by the day. . . .

Well, with all that coming, you'd think our economy would be tanking, our companies would be failing, and our markets would be reeling.

But you'd be wrong. Our economy was shaken, but it is stirring. Our stocks were hurting, but many are hopping. And some of our CEOs were embarrassing, but most were rising . . . to the occasion. And to us.

We proved better than the sum of our fears and the combined wrath of our enemies. We were better than they thought. Maybe even better than we thought.

And on this day, when we honor American labor, I'd go one step further and honor Americans, period. Proving this past year what we should all remember every year—that we're not just a great country because of our ideals, but an even greater country . . . because of our people.

# Now . . . Madrid

*March 15, 2004*

I still can't get the image out of my mind from the attacks on those trains in Madrid. Reports of cell phones ringing on the covered bodies of victims. Some two hundred bodies, many eerily beeping, ringing away. No one answering. No one trying. Frantic relatives praying, wondering where their loved ones were. The day-care worker repeatedly dialing a child's mother. The wife who called hundreds of times, by her count, to hear, finally, that her husband was indeed among the dead.

Little more than four days after the terror, the hurt is still real, the pain still raw, and the anger still palpable. It is understandable for a people torched by terror to do anything in their power to avoid terror. To retrench. And, in the case of the Spanish people, to remake an entire government.

The temptation now is to retreat. Perhaps, they feel, *If we lie low, the terrorists will lay off.*

Terrorists, of course, do not lay off. They seize opportunities and victims where they can find them. They've attacked French tankers. And killed German journalists. Their evil crosses all nationalities and all peoples. Their scourge is indiscriminate, their cruelty indecipherable. They hate for the sake of hating. They kill for the sake of killing. The Spanish today. The Americans' 9/11 earlier. The Indonesians and Malaysians and Australians all those days in between.

Cell phones will continue ringing on the bodies of those who cannot answer. And whose loved ones still look for answers. Then and now. We desperately hope that by avoiding the tiger, we will dodge the tiger, realizing perhaps too late that in so doing, we only end up in the belly of the tiger.

# Capturing a Moment

*July 22, 2004*

Like a lot of dads, I have made a lot of videos of my daughter growing up. Some capture her as just a baby. When I look at them—and I did, a lot, when she started college last year—I just wanted to freeze the moment when she was playing on swings and making a mess of herself eating spaghetti. Some images just do that to you. They make you want to stop the tape. Hold the moment. And not see time move forward.

I had the same feeling watching these latest images from the early morning of 9/11. The five hijackers of American Airlines Flight 77 being screened at Washington's Dulles Airport. Four of them are pulled aside, but later continue on their way. You feel like screaming. *Stop them! They're going to murder people!*

Later they do, by ramming that plane into the Pentagon and killing the plane's forty-seven passengers, six crew members, themselves, and 125 Pentagon employees. But for one moment, we're shown the calm before the storm, desperately hoping we could keep the calm, and lose the storm.

Just like the image of Mohammad Atta frozen in time, going through a Portland Airport security checkpoint to his own World Trade Center date with destiny and death. When these images were taken, 9/11 was still just a date. We were a lot more naïve, a lot more innocent. Images in time are images only for that time.

Just like those of the *Titanic* shipping off nearly a century ago—man's greatest achievement. Unsinkable. Unthinkable. You feel like warning those passengers, warning the crewmembers, warning anyone. . . . *Get off the ship!*

Just like you feel like screaming to the guy driving John Kennedy's car into Dealey Plaza that bright afternoon in Dallas. . . . *Don't make that turn.* But he does make that turn . . . into horror. Into history.

Frozen images frozen in time. The good. The innocent. Before the bad. And the horrible. We know things change. We'd just rather they not. It's why dads hang onto videos of their kids when they were small, and we still cling to images from history when we were safe. As if they'll last forever. Even while we know, deep inside, they do not.

# CHAPTER 2

# *FIGHTING TERROR*

*O*ne of the remarkable aspects of covering the war on terror is how quickly we have forgotten why we're fighting this war in the first place. We had been viciously attacked. I felt it important to keep that in mind. More important, though, I felt it vital to keep our priorities in mind. My goal wasn't to debate whether fighting in Afghanistan or Iraq was a proper response, or even a fair and measured response. My only goal was to point out that the war on evil transcends our times, and defines our times. That's why I have routinely featured on my show the relatives and friends of the victims of that sad day of September 11, 2001. I wasn't trying to mourn their passing, but to remember their passing, and honor the lessons from their passing.

I've said it before, and I'll no doubt keep saying it—I have an obsession with death. I don't mean that in a freakish way, but what I like to call a clear mind way. I think it's vital that, in the day-to-day passing of news—particularly business news—we keep the focus on the business of life, on its beauty and fragility. Throughout the years, that has meant stepping back from the heat of a story and putting it in context, giving it some perspective. I find that much of television news gets caught up in the *moment, without seizing the magnitude behind that moment. Ever since the terrorist attacks on this country, and always mindful of the very real possibility of more horror, I thought— and think—it wise to put our lives in perspective, and to look for reasons to appreciate the country that makes it all possible in the first place.*

## Something Not to Be Proud of, Post 9/11

*May 16, 2002*

Somewhere Osama bin Laden is laughing. Laughing at us. Laughing at how this great, united country isn't quite so united anymore.

I didn't expect the September 11 "Kumbaya" glow to last forever, but I didn't think it would start dissolving so soon. Democrats, who claimed to be in lockstep with the president in the war on terror, now freely question the president in the war on terror. Is he doing too much? Is he doing too little? And now, reports ahead of time. Did he know too much? But do too little?

You can't tell me Osama's not loving this. Assuming he's alive, and I very much think he is, he's got to be thinking, *This is great. They're turning on themselves. They're turning on their leader.* Our enemies love to see us this way. Carping. Ripping. Condemning. Blasting. Second-guessing. And throughout . . . losing. Losing sight of what's important—namely the terror out there, not the bureaucratic snafus here.

Mistakes happened. Oh, if only we all had twenty-twenty hindsight. We feared hijacking, but not this kind of hijacking. We feared bombs, but not box cutters. We feared missiles, but not our own planes. And now we're quite rightly kicking ourselves, but—not rightly—dividing ourselves. Instead of raising a fist, we're waving a finger. Rather than passing the torch, we're passing the buck. Good things can't last forever.

I knew that scene outside the steps of the Capitol—Republicans and Democrats singing the same song—was a Kodak moment. Snap it. And remember it. For soon, some in the picture would forget it.

War is hell. Forgetting we're at war is even more so.

## Back to Butchery

*June 18, 2004*

We know what happened to Paul Johnson. I just hope that eventually the news organizations will show what happened to Paul Johnson. Some discretion is advised. But not too much.

I want the world to see what savages do. I want the world to see what we're up against. Who we're up against. I want the world to see evil for what it is, to compare what happened to some Iraqi prisoners with what happened to some of our prisoners.

I want the world to look closely at the butchered images of Nick Berg . . . and now Paul Johnson. I want the world to try to understand that kind of evil . . . and just try to excuse it. A lot of people can't handle images like this. I can't handle our not trying to handle images like this. I can't handle masking evil. I can't handle not showing planes ramming into buildings, and not showing the gruesome fallout.

There is no nice way to say this, to sugarcoat this. Those who wish us ill have no problem doing horrific things. We should have no problem showing the world their horrific acts. They've made this world a more dangerous place. They want us dead. They want us maimed. They want us no more. The least we could do . . . is return the favor.

# Euro-zeroes!

*April 29, 2002*

Let me see if I've got this straight. The Europeans are angry at us. First for doing too much in the Middle East. Now, apparently, for not doing enough.

No less than *The Economist* editorializes: "George Bush's cavalier approach to foreign policy is one-sided and simplistic." May I offer you an alternative? Do it yourself. If your ideas are so grand, have at it. And get to it. You don't like the way we're trying to negotiate a peace in the Middle East? You try it. You don't like the way we're trying to rid the world of terrorists? You do it. And you don't like the way we carry the world's economic ills on our shoulders? You have a go at it. It ain't easy.

I don't know which is worse—dealing with lethal enemies we can't see or supposed friends we can. Friends who now want to place tariffs on everything from U.S. steel and citrus to rice and clothing. Why, pray tell? Because we had the gall to call their bluff and respond to ridiculously subsidized European steel coming into this country.

I say, *Enough, Europe.* I say, *The next time some terrorists go after you, don't go looking to us. The next time some socialist spender wants to tax you to the wall, don't look to us to foot the bill.*

There are a lot of things we do wrong in this country. And one of them is doing too much for other countries. I don't expect a thank-you. But I certainly don't expect a screw-you. . . . Especially after we give you a hand—and all we get in return is a finger.

## Get Used to It

*January 9, 2002*

Would you rather be inconvenienced . . . or dead?

By now you've heard the story of how Michigan congressman John Dingell had to strip to his skivvies before satisfying airport security officials at Reagan National. And you've no doubt heard about other similar bigwigs who, God forbid, had to suffer the indignities of tighter security.

Folks like New Jersey senator Bob Torricelli, who couldn't get on a flight because he didn't have a photo ID. Or even Secretary of Transportation Norman Mineta, who had to endure a ten-minute search until screeners discovered an aluminum-wrapped Altoid mint. Big hassles. For big guys. And some, pretty embarrassing. But welcome to the new world, guys. Tough for you. Tough for us.

But you know what? As big a pain in the neck as it is, I'd rather be safe and sure than guessing and wondering. I mean, it wasn't that long ago that we were blasting security guys for being too lax, letting people on planes with knives, even guns. Now we're knockin' them for being a bit too protective.

I say, protect away. I know the wait is longer. And it's a pain. I know the crowds are restless. And that's a pain. But I also know that I like being alive. Before I get on the plane, and after I get off the plane. And if that means you want me to strip to my skivvies to make doubly sure of that . . . so be it. Just please do it in a private room.

## Jerusalem. Baghdad. Different Places, Same Terror

*August 19, 2003*

It's horrible enough what happened in Jerusalem today. Yet sadly, innocents getting blown up there is an almost familiar, tragic sight on almost any day.

But I want to focus on another tragedy. I hope the rest of the world took a look at what happened in Baghdad today. Some of their own died there. Good people, trying to do good things in a bad place. The United Nations, which fought this war, is now targeted in this war. An organization dedicated to peace, just the latest victim in this hellish testament to inhumanity.

I wonder now what the world makes of terror that knows no boundaries. Or preferences. Or governments. Or politics. Terror that is indiscriminate. And callous. And evil. Terror that targets those who fight it and those who try to ignore it.

Today we are all awakened by it. Hear me clearly here: We're talking about evil. About people who don't discriminate between paratroopers and peacekeepers. Between those who were finished talking and those who wanted to keep talking. Between those who fought a war and those who did everything in their power to avoid a war.

Terrorists don't care, my friends. Because terrorists aren't our friends. They're monsters. Plain and simple, they are monsters. They'd sooner blow off your head than allow you to get inside theirs. They don't care if you're American, or British, or Israeli, or French, or Spanish, or Indonesian. They don't care what you are, alive. They just want you dead.

And you can't reason with monsters. Any more than you can have a dinner discussion with Hannibal Lecter. Unless you want to end up . . . on his plate.

# Giving Thanks

### *November 27, 2003*

You know what I'm thankful for this Thanksgiving? I'm thankful for the fact that I'm celebrating the day with my family, even though thousands of soldiers are not. I'm thankful that I'm protected over here, because they're watching out for me over there. I'm thankful for a hot meal, even though they'd be thankful for almost any meal. I'm thankful that I'm free to do a job I love, because they're doing a job with bravery that I cannot comprehend.

I'm thankful to see in the eyes of my daughter the great promise of a country made possible by the heroism of a few. I'm thankful that they never waiver, even though many in my profession do. I'm thankful that they love the flag, even though I wonder whether many in my profession ever did. I'm thankful that they can take the heat, while all I have to do is report on the heat. I'm thankful that they're brave, and that I'm just in awe. I'm thankful that they are everything that is right about this country, and that I just cover this country.

I wear fancy suits. They don't. I talk to the financial rulers of the earth. They're stuck fighting the scum of the earth. I'm not fit to judge them, so I won't. But I am fit to thank them, and I will.

To all who defend our freedoms—my freedom—hear this: I couldn't do what I do now, or say what I say now, if you weren't putting it all on the line now. Sometimes it seems like some of us in this country forget that. Let me be the first to say the vast majority of us know that. And know you. And admire you. And thank you.

On a day you should be with your families but you are not. On a day we can be safe at home with our families because you are not.

I'm wise enough to know I've got a good thing going in this country. And I'm grateful enough to know that it's possible because of you guys who are so far from this country this year. That's why it's important to say Happy Thanksgiving. But not nearly as important as saying thanks for just giving.

# CHAPTER 3

# *THE IRAQ WAR*

*N*o sooner had the Iraq War started than I discovered how our collective memories had fogged over. Whatever brief sympathies and support this country enjoyed immediately following the terror attacks, they had long since dissipated by the time of the growing global consternation over our going into Iraq. My goal was not to justify the president's reasoning for extending that war on terror to the footsteps of Saddam Hussein, or to question the infamous weapons of mass destruction as a trigger for doing something sooner rather than later. No, my goal was and is to see this country's fight against evil as the right fight, at just the right time.

Some—make that many—have called me a clueless Yankee Doodle Dandy for merrily trumpeting the U-S-of-A over the rest of the globe. There might be some truth in that. (Bias: I do favor America.) But my greater goal was to give some perspective. I wanted to remind viewers about the unequivocal bias against this country, even in the face of continued reported atrocities aimed at this country, including those people representing this country all over the world.

I'm not saying anything new when I say we are not loved across the globe. I've seen that firsthand. And sometimes we get *what we ask for. Sometimes we are pushy. Sometimes we are de-manding. And often we are a royal global pain. But as I like to remind my audience, we might be a flawed system of government, but we're the best one I know of on this planet. And we've done more good for this planet, helping to free more peoples on this planet, than any other country on this planet. I'm not saying we're owed a thank-you for that, but we're certainly deserving of something more meaningful than a screw-you for that. I find it wise to remind all within earshot the times this country is told the latter, sometimes loudly—but more often, disingenuously quietly, even meekly.*

## In the Face of Terror

*January 30, 2005*

We're still not sure of the exact turnout in Iraq's election today. Seems to be at least 60 percent. Which would be about the percentage of Americans who showed up to vote in our most recent presidential election. But, of course, no one in this country has ever been threatened with death if they voted. No bus of voters was ever blown up. Or polling place obliterated.

No, we voted in peace. They voted in terror. Despite the terror. Despite the warnings. Despite the threats. No, they voted knowing full well the risk they took. And knowing full well that it might have been easier just to stay home. They showed their faces. And they showed their names. They showed the blue ink from voting on their hands. For the world to see. For the terrorists to see. They didn't care. If that doesn't give critics of this whole process pause, I don't know what does.

People must want something pretty badly when they ignore the threat that things could go very badly for them. They must hunger for change, even while risking their own lives for change.

Would we be so gallant in this country? If someone threatened us if we went to the polls, would we go? I wonder. But there's no wondering about what Iraqis did today. The little guy triumphed.

Oh, it'll be a long process. Establishing a freely elected government always is. Especially after what all these people have been through. But in moments when we ask the question, "What did our brave men and women, and many brave Iraqi men and women die for?" I say, the answer is: Look at this day. Savor this day. And remember this day. The day democracy inched forward, and evil took a back seat to something more lasting: hope.

## Living, Not Prospering

*January 24, 2003*

What's more important to you: Your wallet? Or your life? The choice is a bit extreme, of course, but I think your life wins every time. And so it should.

Here's how I see it: It's better to be personally safe than financially stable. That's why I find this piling on about the economy a bit misplaced. We're missing the real battle going on here.

I know this sounds heinous for a business news guy to say, but I think staying alive matters a lot more than staying profitable. The safer we are, the better we are. The more protected

we are, the more profitable we are. Safer nations are more secure nations. It's no accident, as well, that they are more profitable nations. And it's no accident that voters in last year's
mid-term elections ignored doom-and-gloom economic arguments for national security ones.

That's why, for my money, it's not about money. It's about
our security. It's about focusing on what really matters. Not on
each other's stocks, but each other, period.

So the next time someone tells you it's the economy above
all and beyond all, tell them to look at their kids, or their
spouses, or their friends. And ask them this question: "Can you
put a price tag on them?"

Jobs are nice, good jobs are nicer still, but breathing in this
great country is the nicest of all. First things first.


# Remember

### September 24, 2003

He never succeeded at winning over his critics. Some called
him bombastic. Others a warmonger. He warned about terror-
ism. But few listened. He warned about a foreign ogre, but
few seemed to care. He talked of not confronting the enemy.
About the dangers of kowtowing to the enemy. An enemy who
would sooner rip out your heart than let you even think he had
one of his own.

So he prepared for the ogre, and ultimately decided to take
him on. Soon a reluctant world rethought: Maybe this guy was
right about the ogre. Maybe he really is a threat, this ogre fellow. And a great battle ensued. Some were with the ogre. Some

were against the ogre. No matter, the ogre was soon gone. His threat extinguished. And the leader who had been second-guessed was a hero.

But he wasn't a hero for long. Soon, his popularity waned. His support suffered. The realities of rebuilding after a war all but wiped out the glories of winning that war. His fans deserted him. The people who once fell in political lockstep abandoned him. His poll numbers dropped. His people forgot. The man who originally took on terror would later be thrown out of office by the very people who rallied around him because of terror.

I'm not talking about a president named George. I'm talking about a prime minister named Winston. Winston Churchill. This is now, that was then.

Funny thing, history.

## Summer Musings

### July 4, 2003

We barbecue in the sun. They bake in the sun. We swim. They stand watch. We party. They perform. We dither. They deliver. We gather with friends. They gather with comrades. We celebrate our independence. They make it possible. Whether in Iraq or Afghanistan. They protect the peace, so that we can protect this sacred ritual we call the Fourth.

I don't think they'd mind our celebrating. I do think a few would love us remembering what they're sacrificing. What they're giving up. No pool parties for them. No parties, period. Life is tough. And dangerous. But they're focused, and serious. Their comrades are still dying.

So it's worth us all remembering: We're still at war. And they're still fighting that war. They're there, so that we can be here.

My point is not to bring you down, but to make you remember. To make all of us remember. Not just those who serve us bravely there, but those who serve us anywhere. Now, and then. In wars still raging, and wars worth remembering. I'm grateful we have this time to celebrate. I'm even more grateful that we have some pretty brave men and women who are giving us the chance to celebrate. This is their day, this is their moment. This is their cause.

They don't demand much. But they mean so very much.

So let me end by simply saying thank you very, very much. It's the least I can do. After all, I just cover the nation's bottom line. They're the ones battling on the front line. I talk about prices. What they're doing . . . well, that's priceless. Happy Fourth.

## Duty Is as Duty Does

**May 23, 2003**
*(from onboard the USS* Philippine Sea *during Fleet Week)*

If ever you have your doubts about this country, talk to the people who serve this country. People like the ones on board this amazing ship, the USS *Philippine Sea.*

They're incredible men and women. After all they've been through, they smile and joke, kid and dream. They don't earn a lot of money but they sure earn a lot of respect. They don't own much stock, but they sure have me taking stock. And they don't yap about things that make you rich, but live and breathe things that make you think. Like duty. Honor. Country. They do the heavy lifting, while the rest of us do the heavy talking.

While so many were protesting war, they were focusing on winning that war. While some were burning flags, these guys were suiting up so they could. While we debated, they acted. While we went back to our families, they lived for months, far away from their families.

While shows like mine focused on profits, these guys were focused on principles. The freedom we hold dear but don't often talk about. The country we should hold even more dear but rarely brag about.

These are the guys who should be boasting, but won't. These are the guys who should be bragging, but don't.

You know, I talk to a lot of CEOs and cabinet officials, senators and titans. But few mean as much, do as much, or come close to moving me as much as these men, these women, these heroes.

Leave it to a clueless business guy like me to realize on this ship, this day, this moment, that the greatest among us are the ones who are always there for us. Let's remember them. The ones still living. The ones now gone. This is their weekend. Their moment. I've had it with protesters who all but stuck a finger at them. For now, let's all do something far nobler . . . and thank them.

# WMD?

*April 7, 2003*

Have any of you ever heard of the Flat Earth Society? Its members claim the earth is flat, not round. And, satellite images and trips from space not withstanding, they stick to that view.

I used to think flat-earthers were a joke. But they're out there. Apparently, *way* out there. They're the kind of people who won't budge on some firmly held views, no matter what proof you throw at them. As tough as they are, I'm beginning to think they don't have anything on some of these peacenik groups.

Ostensibly, those opposed to the war have said that before we go to war we first need proof that Iraq has chemical weapons. No weapons, no war.

Today, we may have stumbled on plenty of such weapons at a military training camp in central Iraq. Among the stuff U.S. forces uncovered were the nerve agents sarin and tabun, and the blister agent lewisite.

It's still too early to make a big deal out of this. But I see a lot of smoke. A fire's got to be nearby.

Think about this. We now know of al Qaeda training camps working with Iraqi soldiers on the finer points of guerrilla tactics against American forces. We know as well about thousands of gas suits uncovered little more than a week ago in southern Iraq. We know of empty canisters that were thought to have been destroyed years ago, suddenly popping up in Iraq today.

Of course, all of this could be circumstantial. But I have a feeling that, even if it is confirmed, the peaceniks won't budge. Like the flat-earthers, they'll argue for still more proof. More photographs. More chemical sightings.

I suspect I could drive a truckful of sarin to one of their rallies, complete with an Iraqi postmark, and these guys would say it's planted. Look, they don't want war. That's fair. But if that's your motive, quit hiding behind phony reasons.

Because while you're marching, we're uncovering. Unraveling the very reasons you say we shouldn't be in Iraq, and finding a ton of really bad stuff there. Such searches might still amount to nothing. But I know there was a time when Saddam had 'em all, and tried to hide 'em all. Have we since forgotten that all? Can you see anything at all?

Al Qaeda where you said they shouldn't be. And dangerous chemical stuff where you said it wouldn't be.

Maybe you think the earth is flat because you haven't seen it from space. And maybe you think Iraq's on the up-and-up because you want to give 'em space.

You're naïve, or stupid, or both. What will it take for you to put the burning flag down and your head up?

I suspect quite a bit, since first you have to get your head out of another place that seems very dark right now . . . too dark to see anything at all.

## Response to a *New York Times* Critic

*May 13, 2003*

Since no good deed goes unpunished, leave it to the *New York Times* to take a shot at me. Not the *Times* itself, but columnist Paul Krugman, who blasts me for my apparent blatant partisanship. He writes, "Neil Cavuto of Fox News is an anchor, not a commentator. Yet after Baghdad's fall he told 'those who opposed the liberation of Iraq'—a large minority—that 'you were sickening then; you are sickening now.'"

First off, Mr. Krugman, let me correct you. I'm a host *and* a commentator. Just like you no doubt call yourself a journalist *and* a columnist. So my sharing my opinions is supposed to be a bad thing, but you spouting off yours is not?

Exactly who's the hypocrite, Mr. Krugman? Me, for expressing my views in a designated segment at the end of the show? Or you, for not-so-cleverly masking your own biases against the war in a cheaply written column?

You're as phony as you are unprofessional. And you have the nerve to criticize me? Or Fox News? Or by extension, News Corporation?

Look, I'd much rather put my cards on the table and let people know where I stand in a clear editorial than insidiously imply my opinion in what's supposed to be a straight news story.

And by the way, you sanctimonious twit, no one—no one—tells me what to say. I say it. And I write it. And no one lectures me on it. Save you, you pretentious charlatan.

Let me see if I have this right, Mr. Krugman. Journalists who oppose this war are okay, and those who support it are not? Says who? You?

I'm less of a journalist because I was in favor of this war, but you're more of a journalist because you were not?

You imply that by being in favor of this war, I'm pandering—and, by extension, my company is pandering—to the White House. Does it occur to you that I don't have to agree with you? That doesn't make you less of a journalist. But Mr. Krugman, it does make you more of an ass.

Here's the difference. You insinuated it. I just said it. Now I suggest you take your column . . . and shove it.


## Foreign Mockery

*March 25, 2003*

I guess I shouldn't be surprised. No sooner had we encountered some tough fighting in Iraq than our generals were encountering tough questions at briefings.

Is this another Vietnam?

Did we get too cocky?

Are we in too deep?

And here's the one that killed me: Were the French right?

I don't know about you, but I don't remember our guys calling it a video game war. Journalists did. They didn't say Baghdad would be gone in days. Journalists did. They didn't underestimate the power of stubborn Republican guard troops. Journalists did. And they didn't set themselves up to fail. Journalists did.

Let's be clear. War is hell. We owe it to our men and women to appreciate the difference between a high-tech war that looks good on television screens and a very real war that's often too horrible to put on any screen. We know the difference. And I can tell you our soldiers know the difference.

Now some French newspapers have the gall to say, "We told you so." No, all you told us was you didn't want anything to do with rescuing an abused people. But you want everything to do with sharing in the bounty from that rescue. You were phony worms then, you're even phonier worms now.

You're right. War is hell. We knew it going into this. You seemed to have just discovered it now that we're knee-deep in this.

I've had it with all the armchair generals who have no problem taking shots, when there are real generals out there calling the shots, and real soldiers doing the work. I'm not smart enough to judge what they do. But I'm grateful enough to appreciate all they do.

It's amazing that, a week ago at this time, not one shot had been fired. Not one troop had crossed into Iraq. Not one bomb had gone off in Baghdad. Not one tank had moved. Not one B-52 had taken off or F-17 flown. Yet days later, Baghdad's under fire and Basra's under liberation. If this is failure, please show me success.

Why is it so many in my profession would rather say *got ya* . . . than simply muster a *thank ya*?

# What Is Patriotism?

*February 28, 2003*

I always wonder what our troops must be thinking these days. The tens of thousands deployed throughout the Middle East. What do they think of these protests? Or about the Hollywood types who are out there saying we're making a big mistake?

I'll never forget when I was a kid in high school and an army recruiter came for Career Day. As he was leaving the building, someone yelled, "Baby-killer!" The guy stopped momentarily, turned slightly, but then moved on to his car and drove away without saying a word. The Vietnam War was raging at the time, so he was probably used to it. But it bugged me then, and it bugs me now.

I'm not saying you have to be gung ho for the war, but you should be very gung ho about our people who go to war. They're risking their lives so that you can have your marches, and burn your flags, and call your country every name in the book. They're the reason why you have that right. They're the reason I'm here, pontificating on television.

I've never served in the military myself. A quirk of birth, I guess. Too young for Vietnam then, but not too old to feel lucky now. I hope that what I lack in service to my country, I make up for in gratitude to my country. And the people who serve it.

You see, you don't have to be in the parade to appreciate the people marching in it. The husbands, separated from their wives now. The wives, separated from their husbands. The mothers and fathers, apart from their kids. Think of them the next time you call this country names. Think of them the next time you burn a flag. Think of them the next time you call this country a bully. And think of them the next time you talk about sacrifice.

## WMD 2?

*May 5, 2003*

If you can bury bodies, who says it's such a stretch to bury weapons? I began asking myself that question upon hearing, yet again, that they've uncovered still more mass graves in Iraq.

This past weekend, seventy-two bodies were recovered from a shallow mass grave thirteen miles northwest of Najaf. It appears that the victims were lined up and shot. That's all we know.

Here's what else we know: There are other graves. Marines have uncovered several mounds of dirt throughout the area. Local residents were told only a few months ago to avoid these high security areas. Now we know why.

It follows a consistent and numbing pattern. Bodies found in old schools, under a Red Cross hospital, in dilapidated shacks. Bodies hidden then, being unearthed now. Bodies the government insisted weren't there. Just like it said chemical weapons weren't there.

Do you really think that a government that had no problem hiding bodies actually had a problem hiding weapons?

They were pretty good at hiding those bodies. I suspect they were pretty good at hiding those weapons. The only difference is that they didn't have much time to bury those bodies. Some look like they were shot only weeks ago. So Saddam had to move fast. He got sloppy. With the weapons, he had more time.

Yet here's what kills me. So much of the world feigns shock at not having found the weapons—but doesn't say *boo* about finding the bodies. I guess dead bodies are okay. Unrecovered weapons are not.

Here's what I have to say to France and Germany: Remind me again of your priorities. Then look in those graves. What did those people know? What did they see?

They say dead men tell no tales. I disagree. The fact that they are dead—by the hundreds, maybe by the thousands—tells lots of tales. About a government willing to hide them. And God knows what else.

## Smoke and Fire

*February 5, 2003*

What is a smoking gun? Something no doubt many want to see in order to justify going after Iraq.

But what happens when you wait for a smoking gun? By that time, the gun has gone off.

It's smoking, because it has already done something. Which makes me wonder why only then do we react to it. Smoking guns are final events. They're not starting events.

September 11 was a smoking gun. Pearl Harbor was a smoking gun. Hitler going into Poland was a smoking gun. You see? The act of terror *itself* is the smoking gun.

What we ignore are the things that lead to that smoking gun. Like all that al Qaeda noise and the USS *Cole* attack prior to September 11. Like Hitler stomping into lesser countries prior to invading Poland. Like curious ship and troop movements of the Japanese prior to Pearl Harbor.

We always manage to connect the dots after they've forcibly been connected for us. History teaches us it always looks so clear after the fact, after the smoking gun.

After the *Columbia* was destroyed in re-entry, when there had been plenty of warnings about the tiles. After the *Challenger* disaster, when there had been plenty of questions about launching in cold weather.

We never see it coming up until everything we know is blowing up.

Some say where there's smoke, there's fire. I say, by the time you see the smoke, you've missed the fire . . . along with all the other telltale signs you refused to see long before.

# CHAPTER 4

# *FOREIGNERS!*

*M*y father used to say that you could tell the measure of a friend by how he sticks by you, not when things are going well, but precisely when they are not. Sadly, we in the United States have discovered we can count our true friends on barely a hand and a half. Yet when the world has needed us, we've been there. Perhaps I sound like a petulant child when I ask on the air whether we should return the indifference. I'm not trying to be childish, of course. But I am trying to be a realist, because I do hold friends to different standards. Friends owe it to you to stick by you privately, but even at their worst they never speak ill of you publicly.

It's much like a good marriage. A couple may fight in private, but it is the height of silliness to do so in public. What works in personal relationships should work in global ones. I have to wonder, after all these years, why it doesn't.

## They Don't Know Jack!

*June 14, 2001*

*(General Electric chairman Jack Welch's attempts to complete a merger with Honeywell were doomed by an overly protective and overly interfering European Commission. For Welch, it was an*

*unfortunate way to end his career at the top of a great company. But I found it to be a revealing one at that.)*

I feel sorry for Jack Welch. It's hard enough getting U.S. regulators to okay his big merger with Honeywell. Now he's burning up his frequent flier miles trying to get Europeans to OK it as well. Good luck.

He might end up having to give up so much that he might wonder why he made the deal in the first place.

More than a few of you have claimed that I'm a little insular on these matters, so please, tune out now. Because I'm getting on my soapbox again.

Here's what slays me: The Europeans telling us that the deal is anticompetitive.

You gotta be kidding. That would be like me lecturing someone for buying too many cannoli in a bakeshop! Hmmm . . . fat chance.

In what I can only describe as the highest case of international chutzpah, the Europeans are calling Jack a bully. That GE and Honeywell together would dominate the aerospace and automation markets—that no one else would have a chance.

Please. What do you call Airbus?

Here's what I call it. A government program, fully subsidized and protected by Europe's strongest governments. Times get tough, Airbus gets help. You think Boeing gets breaks like that in this country? I don't think so.

We have this silly notion called competition. And I think that some in Europe are afraid of it. And for good reason. Competition strikes at the very chord of the cradle-to-grave protection many European workers are afforded by their governments.

That kind of security is nice. I just don't think it's realistic. Or that we should pay for it. I'm not saying this because I like Jack Welch or his Honeywell deal. I am saying it because I don't like hypocrites judging that deal.

Oh, you earnest European Commission judges, just be honest when you say you don't like it. Say that it threatens you. Scares you. And maybe forces you to change your ways. For all I know, GE and Honeywell may be big bullies. But I know an even bigger one. And, Europe, so do you.

## Where Are Our Friends?

### December 11, 2003

One of my favorite things to do each morning when I get into work is peruse the foreign press. I like to know what they think of us. Apparently not much.

The latest fuel for their anti-U.S. fire is the issue of Iraqi contracts. The White House's position is that only coalition-supporting countries need apply. The French called that arrogant. Of course, the French calling anyone arrogant is like me chastising someone for not eating a salad. . . .

But I digress. The Germans called President Bush cavalier. The Belgians, selfish. South Korea says we're sending the wrong message. And so on.

Sometimes when I get a little tired, I get a little blunt. It's a good thing I'm not the president of the United States. Because I'd just snap.

I'd tell the Germans who don't like our thousands of troops there: All right, I'm pulling them out.

I'd tell the French who don't like our conflict intervention: The next time you get a butcher from Bosnia, you have at it.

I'd tell the South Koreans: If we're such an annoyance protecting your sorry asses from that nut in the pajamas just north of you, you deal with the nut in pajamas. We'll sit this one out.

Frankly, I'm sick and tired of countries that say they're sick and tired of us.

If you hate us so much, do without our dollars. Do without our troops. Do without our aid. And our support and our security. And our help. Do without those things you know you can't live without.

We're not a perfect country. But I'll tell you what—we're not a smarmy, wormy, backstabbing, double-crossing, second-guessing, two-bit, butt-licking, phony country. What you see is what you get.

So, Jacques, the next time some butcher's at your doorstep and you come screaming to us for help, don't be surprised if we take a pass and suggest you take a stand.

I won't hold my breath waiting for that headline.

## Thanks for Nothing, Kuwait

*February 16, 2000*

Talk about ungrateful! Because I'm talking about Kuwait.

You remember the country, right? We saved its butt from Saddam Hussein some years back. And guess what?! Lo and behold, it turns out Kuwait's one of the big OPEC guys refusing to budge on its oil production to bring prices down.

Excuse me? Did I hear this right? You want to keep prices high? Maybe have 'em go higher? And maybe have us keep paying those higher prices?

Us—the same folks who made sure you didn't become a travel stop on the way to Baghdad? The same folks who organized a global force unprecedented in history to save your pathetic oil-soaked state? The same folks who risked life and limb when you came crawling to us with one plea: "Help us!"

Well, pardon me for being so blunt. But you've got nerve.

You wouldn't even be around as a country if it wasn't for this country. Yet you treat this country as if—well, as if we weren't even this country. A country that picked you up, cleaned you up, and set you up . . . apparently just to screw us up.

Well, thanks a lot.

Oil prices are back to where they were when Saddam was just marching on your sorry doorstep. Back then, we stopped him. Knowing what we do now about you, I wonder if we should have.

Maybe I'm overreacting, but I know I'm not overreaching when I say you're like the spoiled-rotten kid whose parents doted on him all growing up. He doesn't call. He doesn't write. He doesn't come for the holidays. That upsets parents. And this upsets us.

I don't know which is worse—that you're doing this, or that you don't even care that you're doing this.

## If in France, Pack!

*February 18, 2003*

You know, I prattle on a lot about the French, but sometimes they make it almost too easy. I mean, did you hear the latest?

French president Jacques Chirac has been ripping—and I mean ripping—Eastern European nations who signed letters last month backing the U.S. position on Iraq.

Chirac said, "It is not really responsible behavior. It is not well brought up behavior."

But here's the kicker. His last little snit: "They missed a good opportunity to keep quiet."

All right, Jacques, let me see if I've got this right. It's perfectly all right to hear from countries that support your do-no-harm view on Iraq, but God forbid one of these lesser members speaks out.

You pathetic political twerp. You think you're better than Poland, or Hungary, or Romania, or Bulgaria, or the Czech Republic? That they have no right to air views that dare conflict with your own?

I think a lot of those guys know what it's like to be under totalitarian regimes. They know what ogres can do. I would think you would too. But enough of me. Back to you, you sniveling backstabbing phony.

Now, you're threatening these countries' entry into your elite club, the European Union? What's the matter? Afraid you might be losing your influence? Or just afraid your new partners might come to realize you never had any to begin with?

It's amazing. You scold us for being hostile to criticism, yet you can't deal with it in your own backyard. Jacques, you say you're full of hope for peace. I say, you're full of *crepe*.

## Judge Not Ahnold!

*August 12, 2003*

So I'm driving home, listening to this radio discussion featuring foreigners commenting on Arnold Schwarzenegger's run for California governor. I think they included a couple of French guys, some woman from England, and a teenager from Germany. Almost universally, they were amused.

The British woman actually said something like, "That's America, for you. Silly stuff."

The French dudes were even worse. They said it made this country look like a laughingstock.

Oh, really?

Well, *messieurs*, you may have a problem with the fact that a couple hundred people have declared themselves candidates to run the biggest state in the United States. But I don't.

You may say they've made a mockery of the process. But I don't. I say they've restored the fun in the process.

You may think Californians are nutty. But I don't. Those nuts have created the fifth largest economy in the world. Larger than your sorry, Chablis-sipping socialist selves, I might point out.

You may think it vulgar that a stripper runs for office. But I don't. In this country, anyone can run for office.

And you may think you have the market cornered on good government. But I don't agree. Because I'd much rather take a stripper, an actor, and a comedian and have them duke it out, than a lifelong pol, a socialist, and bureaucrat debating what cradle-to-grave government programs should win out.

You might call our process silly and comical. I call your arrogance obnoxious and revolting.

You might wallop the state of our affairs. I'd take any of our states over any of your affairs.

Because at least in this country, we lay it all out. Given all your desperate economies, it seems that some of you foreigners have yet to figure anything out.

I'd sooner see an actor take a shot at leading than a social-ist take a shot at any of us governing.

We're not perfect. I'm just glad we're not you.

# United Waste of Time!

*July 3, 2003*

So let me see if I have this right. The UN needs us. Not in Iraq, where it argued we shouldn't go. But in Liberia, where it argues we *should* go. Liberia's a mess and needs to be stabilized, the UN says. Funny, Iraq was a mess but apparently didn't need to be stabilized, the UN said. Why quibble over the details?

The administration is indeed sending at least a thousand GIs to Liberia. Maybe double that number down the road. Part of a global peacekeeping force that needs some clout. And we just provided it. We could have said, the hell with your request. But we didn't.

We could have ignored the desperate pleas from Liberians looking to end a civil war that's already claimed hundreds of lives. But we didn't.

We could have been vindictive and said to the French and Germans—who led this request, by the way—"You didn't do diddly for us, and we ain't doing diddly for you." But we didn't.

No, we recognized the greater good by doing some good. Uncle Sam to the rescue again.

You know, there are a lot of things wrong. But when every-thing hits the fan, we do one thing right. We calm people. We protect people. We save people.

Sometimes I wonder why we do anything for fair weather friends who hate us one moment, and then dizzily come running to us the next. Then I look back in our history and I realize it's because we've done the exact same thing before, time and time again. Not bad for a country that the world loves to hate. Until the world is scared to move.

## French Whine

*June 5, 2003*

A French viewer weighs in on my weighing in on that global survey that bashes the United States. Louis B. from Paris, France: "You call us ungrateful. We call you arrogant. Look in the mirror. You're the face of a boob nation."

Hey, Louis . . . look up the definition of arrogant. It's moved in the dictionary. It's under "ungrateful." You know what arrogant is, Louis?

Arrogant is having the gall to say we don't listen to opposing views when you're not hearing any but your own.

Arrogant is saying we're bullies when you're the one whose country tried to strong-arm Bulgaria and Latvia out of your precious European club.

Arrogant is acting open but being sneaky, Louis.

Arrogant is sending your ambassador to arm-twist African UN members to vote your way and stick it to us.

Arrogant is saying you abhor military conflicts while sending nuclear technology to a despot who had only military intentions.

Arrogant is forgetting people who were with you, Louis, when no one else was.

Arrogant is taking our money, then stabbing us in the back.

Arrogant is worming your way into a freed Iraq, when you didn't shed one drop of blood to see that freedom.

Arrogant is sneering at a country that suffered and took action, while you debated and did nothing.

Arrogant is clueless. And cunning.

Arrogant is saying you love us, when you only want to screw us.

Arrogant is acting like you care when you don't. And insisting you're being above board when you are not.

Arrogant is dismissive. Arrogant is deceitful. And arrogant, Louis, is you.

I'm not going to give you dietary tips. Don't even think of giving me moral ones.

You're right, we're not popular. But I'll tell you this . . . at least we're not worms.


# Them Against Us!

*June 4, 2003*

I hate to break it to you, but the world doesn't flip over this country, my friends. The latest proof is an exhaustive twenty-nation survey of some sixteen thousand people put out by the Pew Research Center that confirms what I've long suspected: We ain't liked.

It goes from contempt in Jordan, where only 1 percent of those surveyed expressed a favorable opinion of the United

States, to mild hatred in Indonesia and Turkey, where 15 percent felt the same way, to general distrust in Germany and France.

Big surprise.

But here's the kicker. In Indonesia, Jordan, and the Palestinian authority, more people had confidence in Osama bin Laden to "do the right thing in world affairs." You've got to be kidding me!

Majorities in NATO countries want less dependence on the United States. They don't like us. Call it the war. Call it President Bush's cowboy style. Call it whatever you want, they want to see and hear less of us.

I say, have it your way. You don't like us? You don't have to put up with us.

Indonesia, you have no problem with Osama bin Laden? Give him a call after the next terrorist attack in your country, courtesy of Osama bin Laden.

Germany, you don't flip over our troops in your country? So protect your own damn country.

France, you think we're too heavy-handed? Don't look to us the next time you need a hand.

NATO friends, don't like our NATO influence? Try doing without our NATO money.

Arab friends, don't think much of our going after a despot threatening the world? Let's see what you do the next time a despot threatens your part of the world.

You say we're too focused on terror? See what you would do if terrorists were focused on flying planes into your buildings, and killing your people, and scaring your kids.

You have problems with our country, but you seem to have no problem with our money.

I'm not saying you have to like us. But consider very seriously what some of your own ungrateful lives would be like without us.

# Three Stooges

*April 12, 2003*

Let me ask you something. Do you remember Larry, Curly, and Moe? I'd like to introduce you to Jacques, Gerhardt, and Vladimir.

Larry, Curly, and Moe were pretty funny. Jacques, Gerhardt, and Vladimir are pretty funny too. But Larry, Curly, and Moe were just joking around. Jacques, Gerhardt, and Vladimir are not.

Larry, Curly, and Moe made you love their antics. Jacques, Gerhardt, and Vladimir make you wonder about their antics.

Larry, Curly, and Moe had no agenda but to make you laugh. Jacques, Gerhardt, and Vladimir have a very serious agenda . . . but they only end up making us all laugh.

Only stooges who did nothing to free an oppressed people would smarm their way in to profit off those people.

Only stooges who tried desperately to protect an evil regime would come out and say they're glad the world's not done with that regime.

And only stooges would ignore the pain of families who've lost loved ones in this worthy battle and call it a waste, while sticking it in the eyes of those same families to make new contracts with great haste.

The original Three Stooges tickled us. The new three stooges sicken us. The original Three Stooges lifted us up when we were down. The new three stooges bring us down when we are up.

The original Three Stooges knew they were stooges and laughed all the way to the bank. The new three stooges have no clue they're stooges, but still want to run to the bank. Only this bank, this day, is closed.

We're onto their thievery as much as we are their stoogery. Larry, Curly, and Moe are an institution. Jacques, Gerhardt, and Vladimir should be in one.

# Friendly Fire

*March 18, 2003*

I do find it interesting that ever since we announced an ultimatum to Iraq, there's been a lot of backpedaling from our so-called friends. France is volunteering to help us rebuild. And Germany is saying they always loved the United States.

Out countries want in. Turkey's scrambling to offer room for our troops. Russia's just trying to stay quiet. Before long, I half expect Belgium to send our soldiers chocolates.

It's amazing what a little decisiveness can do. Suddenly fence-sitters become armchair helpers. I just hope this country has a good memory. That we won't forget how so many other countries left us high and dry. How the Germans, of all people, had the gall to call us militaristic. How the French called us duplicitous. How they flew around Africa, literally trying to buy off countries to block us. And now they're feeling blocked. And now they're worried. Very worried.

What will happen to their deals? And their contracts? And their business commitments in the Gulf?

I know a place they can put those deals, and those contracts, and those commitments. But this being a family show, I'll stay quiet.

It's amazing that these guys think we're dumb enough to forgive and forget. They know us well. We're so decent that we do forgive, and we do forget.

Me? Sadly, I'm a tad more vindictive. I remember the ones who said they were my friends and then proved it. I remember more the ones who said they were my friends . . . and then did not.


# One More!

*September 22, 2004*

Is it me, or are these UN guys just asking for it?

I wasn't too far from the UN last night for an event I had to attend. Some of the streets nearby were closed off. One visibly ticked-off UN delegate proceeded to tell the policeman, "You don't realize who I am. I must get through."

The policeman responded, "I don't care who the hell you are, pal, no vehicles allowed."

He persisted as a line was developing. "Get these people out of my way. I'm very late," he bellowed. By now he was creating a scene.

The officer asked for ID from anyone waiting to drive through. The UN guy was insulted. He demanded his driver flash his parking pass.

"Not good enough," the officer said.

Apparently security was extra tight. The president was staying at the Waldorf Astoria, not too far away.

By now, this knucklehead was apoplectic. He stormed out of the car and practically barreled into me. Mind you, he was about my size, so I was thinking the walk would do us both good.

Now he was fuming—shouting at his assistant something about being very late for a dinner, saying (I kid you not), "Remove these people from my way!" So the assistant, all of eighty pounds and approximately the size of my arm, gamely tried to clear a path with all the force of Tinkerbell at a World Wrestling event. I didn't know whether to hit the guy or swat him. No one moved. No one cared. Most laughed. And we all continued on our way.

But all that time I was thinking: My tax dollars are supporting this clown? Never mind that these guys don't have to pay parking tickets. They could practically get away with murder and not be penalized. And they have the nerve to complain about the very security meant to protect boneheads like themselves? Me? I've got to admit, I walked extra slow. And made it extra hard for this guy to pass. Yes, I was the ugly American. But last night, I was enjoying every minute of it.

## April Fools'

*April 1, 2003*

When you're wrong, you're wrong. And when it comes to the French, I was wrong. You heard me right. I've blasted them too much. And now I realize I went too far.

I called them ingrates for ripping us on Iraq when we helped them through so many wars. They have told me it's precisely because they're grateful and that they're trying to encourage us to avoid other wars.

I offered a few choice places they could stick their wine and cheese. They never, not once, told me where I could stick my Yodels.

I said they were more interested in protecting buildings than they are in protecting principles. They responded that when you value the things that look good, you are doing good.

They said I struck from the gut, and not the head. They were right. I was way too emotional. And more often way too strident. They remained the utmost of decorum. And dignified. I was more shoot-from-the-hip, and far from dignified. They see this war on this day as proof that great countries can make great mistakes.

I see this day for what it is.

April Fools'.

Gotcha.

## CHAPTER 5

# *HONOR, DUTY, COUNTRY . . . GRATITUDE*

*P*erhaps there is no group of Americans I hold in higher regard than those who have served and continue to serve this country. I remember one Fox-bashing e-mailer once wrote, "Neil, for a guy who never served himself, you spend a heck of a lot of time talking about those who do."

That's precisely the reason. I never forget for one single day that the good fortune I've enjoyed in life is because of the sacrifice others have made in their lives—sometimes surrendering their lives in the process. My dad saw the horrors of war up close during "The Big One," as he called it: World War II. When I asked him whether he ever thought of not serving, he seemed surprised, even taken aback. "It was just the thing to do," he told me. "It was the only thing to do."

He's long gone now, but not a day goes by that something doesn't remind me of his simple humility and courage. He and his generation are the links to an era of decency I have long aspired to, but fall woefully short emulating. Nevertheless, not having served doesn't mean not serving respect toward those who do.

*It's why I've argued many times that simply because you don't march in the parade doesn't mean you can't stand back on the sidelines and salute those who do.*

*I never had the opportunity to serve. And I've grown to admire those who didn't and don't wait to be called, but call upon themselves to serve and be counted. They are far greater than I. It's why I never forget to thank them, and never, ever, ever forget to honor them.*

## We Hardly Knew Ye

*November 11, 2002*

Did you ever catch a story that just made you think? This one's off the Associated Press. There's a national cemetery in Bushnell, Florida, that's been pretty busy lately, burying upwards of thirty veterans a day. Every day. Tomorrow, more than forty funerals are scheduled.

Most of those caskets hold World War II vets, now dying at a rate of nearly one thousand a day in America alone. *One thousand a day.*

The greatest generation is leaving us. And fairly quickly.

There's the story of seventy-four-year-old veteran Al Williams, who says simply, "Sometimes it gets to you. . . . I've lost a lot of friends." His honor guard alone handles five funerals a day.

Florida seems a long way from places like Normandy, and Iwo Jima, and Dresden, but Florida is where so many of these heroes went to close out their storied lives. The last chapter in their lives.

And one by one, they leave us, but a tad more rapidly now than before.

As cemetery director Bill Murphy puts it, "They're coming through these gates from the time we start in the morning until we finish at 2:30 P.M."

And then all over again the next day. Until, by 2008 or maybe 2010, it all crawls to a trickle . . . and then a stop. The greatest generation gone. Quietly. Almost invisibly.

A generation that made so much noise for the world to hear is stepping off the stage silently now, sadly now, with dignity now.

They made our world a more secure place. I trust and pray they have found an even better place. God knows, they're entitled.

Happy Veterans Day. And thank you.


# Military Ballots

### November 22, 2000

I received hundreds upon hundreds of e-mails concerning my military ballot commentary this week. You might recall that I believe these ballots should be counted regardless of their condition, whether they're stamped, or postmarked, or pock-marked, or . . . whatever. The overwhelming majority of you agreed. But some of you felt I was the wrong guy to be championing the military cause.

I disagree. I think I'm exactly the right guy. No, I did not serve. I never had to. When I was of age, no wars were ensuing, no crises building, no draft or lottery was going.

But just because I didn't serve doesn't mean I don't admire those who do. And those who did. In fact, it makes me all the more grateful for them, and much more concerned about them. Maybe because they did and do the heavy lifting for me. Maybe because I admire heroes. Or maybe because I've learned to be grateful, and am willing to admit that I'm damn lucky, because of these folks.

So when I say cut 'em some slack and let their ballots count, I damn well mean it. This isn't a dimple issue or chad issue. This is an American issue.

These guys aren't voting for just a president. They're voting for their commander and chief—a guy whose orders mean life and death.

Think about that.

Then think about the forty-four ballots of theirs that are rejected for no postmark, or the thirty-seven for an invalid postmark, or the sixteen scrapped because of no witness signature.

Please. Enough.

Anyone risking life and limb thousands of miles away from home deserves leeway. I know this sounds crazy, but they are better. A cut above the rest of us . . . certainly a cut above me.

So I say this: If you're going to allow a chad to count, count the real Chads . . . and Bobs, and Toms, and Pams, and Barbaras . . . the men and women of our military who vote and hope the system counts their votes.

I'm not taking a Republican side, or Democratic side. I think I'm taking the American side.

And as the son of a veteran, all I ask is that as we serve up the fixings, let's serve up the courage to say thank you. After all, they're the reason we're sitting down to dinner in the first place.

# Ronnie

### June 7, 2004

The greatest generation gasped this past weekend. Ronald Reagan passed away on Saturday. Perhaps the final throng to commemorate D-day on Sunday. Both harkened back to a different time. A different moment. A time when men spoke little, but did much. When what they did say, they did mean.

When my mom was alive, she loved Ronald Reagan. Perhaps owing to her Irish ancestry, she used to call him her generation's last gasp. Reagan is simply the most prominent of that generation to recently pass. He is not the last.

There's the story of how Ronald Reagan refused to take off his jacket in the Oval Office, even on one day when it was especially hot. "Not here," he would say. "Not in this room."

At this time, I harken back to their time. When a man held a door open for a woman, and another man talked of morning in America. They were a grand generation that spoke to our qualities without really speaking at all.

My mother is gone now. And my father, too. And so many of that generation. And now, Ronald Reagan, too. One by one, hero by hero, good soul by good soul. Surrendering the good fight we call life.

Remembering the good, epic battle we called World War II. One weekend. One week. When we reflect on what we had . . . and what a wonderful generation did.

# Memorial Day

*May 25, 2000*

It's already started. Actually, it started weeks ago. The ads. Tons of 'em. Memorial Day sales. They're everywhere. A chance for shoppers to get bargains. And then barbecue.

Memorial weekend. The traditional kickoff of summer. Everything seems timed around this three-day event. Big movies, like *Mission Impossible II*. And big pool parties, maybe one in your own backyard. It's a happy time. And so it should be.

I think a lot of us work pretty hard. We deserve a holiday. I just hope that some of us take a little time to reflect on what Memorial Day is really all about. Not red tag sales. But reflection.

A chance to ponder those who've gone before us, who sacrificed for us, and all those creature comforts we hold so dear.

Trust me, I'm not interested in ending this show on a downer. But I do want to slow things down a bit . . . to remember those who gave their lives so that we may enjoy ours.

I'm talking about our veterans of all wars. Some controversial. But all noble, very noble.

Think about how much we owe to the guys who died, so that we may shop, and barbecue, and gather with our friends. I don't think one of them would mind that. I think they'd be happy for that. And for us.

They helped secure all we hold so dear. I guess all they'd ask is to give them just one passing thought—an acknowledgment that what they did mattered then, and matters now.

This country has grown to be the most powerful, most envied on earth. A lot of men and women gave their lives for this powerhouse. Some of their comrades are still with us. Many feeble now. Some bitter now. But all important now.

Enjoy these good times. They would welcome that. But enjoy their memory, too. Because they would welcome that even more.

## Flag Pin

*June 14, 2002*

This being Flag Day and all, I thought I'd pass along a letter I received from a viewer, Thom M., who writes, "I notice I still see flag pins on you and some of your Fox cronies. It's getting a little old, don't you think? It's also getting a little over-the-top. How can you question or critique your government when you march like lemmings to its every pronouncement?"

Well, Thom, first things first. I'm not here to judge people who don't wear flag pins. So why judge those who do?

Patriotism isn't determined by a pin. It's determined by the heart that beats behind that pin.

Free speech advocates seem to make a bigger deal out of protecting the rights of those who burn a flag than those who simply wear one. But no matter.

Loving one's country and loving one's job are not incompatible. Just like being a good American and a good journalist are not inseparable. I can be a harsh critic of what this country does wrong. Wearing a flag pin doesn't make me any less so.

But you're quite right on one crucial issue, Thom. I am biased. I do love my country. And I am proud of my country. And as a journalist, I'm proud of what this flag represents to me and what it offers for me. The chance to criticize it, analyze it, debate it, even condemn it.

Ironically, the very journalists who love to leap on anything this country does wrong, also refuse to acknowledge the simplest protections for everything they want to do right.

I've said it before. I'll say it again: I'd rather be a good person than a good journalist. A good American than a good wordsmith.

I don't judge those in my profession by what they wear. I do judge them by what they say. Not whether there's a pin over their heart, but whether they even have a heart.

Me? I wear my emotions on my sleeves, and yes, my lapel. You say it's all because of September 11, Thom. Maybe you're right. Up until then, I took everything I had for granted. Since then, I leave nothing to chance. Like the chance to say, I'm lucky. And I'm grateful.

You say when my show comes on, you switch me off. It's a free country, Thom. Just as I'm free to tell you, go ahead.

## CHAPTER 6

# "DON'T BE A SMART ASS!"

*I*t was August 1980. I had just graduated from college and finished a summer-long fellowship program at the Indianapolis
News. Armed with clippings from that fine newspaper and eager
to make a go of it in financial journalism, I stepped into the New
York offices of Crain Communications, where an amiable Aus-
tralian editor by the name of Michael Clowes was to interview
me about a Washington reporter opening at Pensions & Investments Age, a trade paper for the pension community. The job
didn't sound sexy, but the locale did. I loved Washington and
thought it would be fun to get in on the ground floor there, any
way I could.

Michael was one of the nicest people I had met, or ever would
meet, in the business. He readily understood my business naiveté,
but appreciated my eagerness. He questioned me about the presidential race that was raging between incumbent Jimmy Carter,
who was ahead in the polls, and this guy Ronald Reagan, who
was beginning to move up. He reminded me that if Reagan got in,
there'd be big changes coming. Wall Street would fundamentally
change too, he told me, and Washington itself would be "Ground
Zero" for this revolution that he seemed convinced was coming. I

*remember blurting out something stupid like, "I can't see this Reagan guy winning. He scares too many people."*

*"Just watch him in the debates," Mike said. "You'll be surprised, and I think Americans will be surprised, at just how good and just how presidential this guy is." Mike was right, of course, but the interview itself was a mind-bending process. He threw so many facts and figures at me! I think he was disappointed that I didn't grasp the material with the same zeal he did—or, for that matter, that I didn't already know everything he was talking about. When he was referring to people's portfolios, I thought he was talking about pocketbooks. (Little did I realize then that I wasn't too far off the mark.)*

*I was green. I was stupid. But I got the job. And I got it not so much for what I knew, but precisely for what I did not. Michael told me he'd always be there to explain things, as long as I took the time to explain things to the readers, too. He was insistent on that, reminding me that all too often journalists talk over readers' heads. Acronyms get built into copy and conversation, so much so that you wonder for whom the copy is being written in the first place. Even though* Pensions & Investments Age *was a trade publication geared to the professional investment crowd, Michael never took advantage of that, or assumed that his writing or the publication's writing should be geared toward that.*

*"Explain everything," he told me again and again. Every good publication worth its editorial salt did the same. True enough, no less than the* Wall Street Journal *always defines routine jargon and business parlance. I suspect the average* Journal *reader knows full well what price-earnings multiples are all about, and understands even esoteric terms like cash dividend yields—yet each time such a term is used in its pages, it's explained. The best journalists, I realized, don't flaunt their knowledge. They share it. And that's a fundamental difference.*

It's what I've tried to do throughout my financial reporting, and later political reporting life; first because I had to, later because I wanted to, and always because my readers and viewers expected me to.

Business shows today are taken as boring, as if the news itself were boring. It isn't. If you report things the same old way, with the same old jargon, and the same old numbing repetition of data, you'll lose people. My boss, Roger Ailes, knew this from the start with my show on Fox, changing the title to Your World, to reflect the ubiquitousness of news, business included.

Roger hates pompous people almost as much as my dad did when he was alive. This high-school-only educated man, who became pretty successful in life, frequently reminded his son, "It's all right to be smart. It's not all right to be a smart ass."

As I accumulated more education, he also warned me not to accumulate the baggage that often comes with it—including arrogance. "There's only one thing worse than an asshole," he'd impolitely put it, "and that's a college-educated asshole."

I don't think Roger—or my dad—would be much impressed by the tone and tenor of a lot of news anchors and reporters today. I certainly know Roger doesn't much like elitists, who love acting like elitists. Roger likened it to a club, and a club with a members-only conversation.

That's why with every news item I try to tell a story, to put the news of the day in some perspective, so that people at home can grasp its meaning and appreciate its bigger context. I often use humor, but always to make a serious point.

That was the case back in the late 1990s when a booming economy was the story of the day. I tried to step back—sometimes to warn, other times to relate what was happening in those days.

*The huge budget surpluses we were racking up at the time were getting a great deal of attention. Every one seemed to be saying that deficits, and eventually our massive debt itself, would all be things of the past. I wasn't quite so sure, just as I wasn't quite so sure that the enormous run-up in the stock market at the time might not be based on an unhealthy logic that ignored fundamentals, like history. My goal wasn't to be a wet blanket, but to provide some pause to the panting.*

*In the following pieces, I tried to showcase the issue of the day, be it a booming economy or a booming market or a booming interest and passion for anything technology-related. All of these were the rage at one time or another. And at that time I tried to get inside their magic. What made people so passionate about them? So zealous? And yes, so crazy?*

*Again, my goal was not to dismiss the rage, but to understand the logic behind the rage. Sadly, sometimes, I discovered that the passion was everywhere, but the logic virtually nowhere. To back up my views, I often relied not on statistics, but on lessons far more enduring—lessons provided by family members who are long gone, but whose wisdom is not forgotten. I figure there's no better way to capture the mood of the moment, even the poster issue of the moment, than with a story—even a self-deprecating one.*

## How the Mighty Fall

### September 25, 1998

I think I know why I never quickly raised my hand in class. A lot of it had to do with the simple fact I didn't know what was going on. The way I figured it, why risk looking foolish?

That's the danger of being the smartest kid in the class, or pretending to be. You set up unrealistic expectations. People start to think you really are that smart. Disappoint them, and you devastate them.

Take John Merriweather's humbling moment. He's the brainiac behind Long-Term Capital Management, the big hedge fund that has just failed big time.

I gotta tell ya: John failing is like Moses getting caught in a Clinton-Monica deal. You just don't see it. When he was a hot-shot bond trader at Salomon Brothers, colleagues called him infallible. In *Liar's Poker,* he was deemed God-like. He had a knack for hedging tiny price differences in bonds across the globe. Instant money. Instant recognition. And for Mr. Merriweather, instant fame.

It brought instant investors, too, when he went out on his own. All convinced this smart guy could do no wrong. So they ponied up ten million dollars a pop to be in his club, only to end up getting clubbed.

The fact that he had two Nobel Prize–winning economists joining him only added insult to injury. How could folks who were so smart be so dumb? They lived by their marketing. And ultimately suffered from the hype of that marketing. It's enough to make future geniuses take pause. And maybe not raise that hand in class.

## Too Easy Money?

*January 29, 1999*

I've asked this question before, but it bears asking again. If you woke up one morning and suddenly discovered you had thousands of dollars more in your account than you thought, what would you do? Would you spend it right away? Or hang on to it, for fear that it couldn't be right?

It's a timely question for this country—because, in case you didn't hear, we're collectively rolling in the dough. According to the Congressional Budget Office, budget surpluses will total $2.6 trillion over the next decade, far more than anyone expected.

Here's the humdinger, though: it used to be that the big reason we had extra cash was that, for now at least, we're pouring a lot more into Social Security than we're taking out. That'll change very soon, mind you, but those Social Security surpluses have been a godsend.

But here's the kicker: It turns out that, even without that retirement dough, we're likely taking in nearly eight hundred billion bucks more than we're spending through the year 2009. How tempting: Republicans want tax cuts. Democrats want to save Social Security. Lots of folks in between want to do all of the above.

Enter Alan Greenspan, who says, *Hold your horses. These are estimates, as quick to change as a recession is to form.* I guess Al's the guy who sees the dough and argues with the bank that it ain't *his* dough, until he knows for sure. The rest of Washington clearly isn't concerned, not by a long shot, and that's what worries me.

## Let the Good Times, Not the Facts, Roll!

*February 2, 1999*

Have any of you ever tried to make a budget? It's not easy, right? After all, if you're paying out more than you're taking in, that's generally not good. Budgets help set you straight.

Let's say you discover that you eat out an awful lot—maybe three, four times a week. So you slash that down to twice, to save some dough.

Or maybe you're a clotheshorse, doling out 20 percent more each year on what you wear than you make. Again, not good.

But what if you could change what you make—the income side of the ledger, if you will. What if you factored in not a paltry 3 percent cost-of-living increase, but 10 percent or more? Suddenly, you wouldn't have to cut spending on those sweaters or steak dinners.

That's kind of the position Uncle Sam finds himself in now. Since he's had a good run, taking in a lot of dough, he figures he'll keep rolling in that dough. He says it's likely to yield nearly three trillion smackers in extra cash over the next fifteen years.

It's the "likely" part that troubles me, because Uncle Sam's factoring in 10 percent annual returns in the stock market, and interest rates remain obscenely low. All of that just might happen. But banking on the good stuff instead of cutting the hard stuff is wishful stuff. You may be right. And lucky. But like you and me at home, you're more likely wrong. And in the red.

## Buy Now! Think Later!

*April 22, 1999*

I'm convinced we are judged not so much by what we do, but by what others think we'll do. I know that's a mouthful, but my point is this: Expectations are everything.

If people think you're a jerk, and you end up being very pleasant, you're doubly popular.

If people think you're pleasant, and you end up acting like a jerk, you're doubly unpopular.

Guys in the stock market play much the same game. They base their bets, essentially, on how companies will perform. Let's say you think a company is going to make a hundred million dollars in the quarter, and it makes two hundred million bucks. Well, you don't have to be an Einstein to figure out that the stock of that company is going to jump because its profits were a lot stronger than anyone thought.

And, right about now, a lot of companies are reporting profits that are generally a lot stronger than these smarty-pants analysts thought they would be. In fact, less than halfway through the first quarter, more than a third of the earnings we're getting are beating Wall Street estimates.

That's why Wall Street scored a record again, up more than 145 points to within spitting distance of 11,000 on the Dow Jones Industrials, buoyed by issues like IBM that more than wowed 'em.

But here's the problem I have with some of these expectations. They're based on numbers revised downward by the corporations themselves. Sort of like me telling my mom and dad to brace themselves for Cs and Ds on my report card, only to be pleasantly surprised by a couple of Bs.

Never mind that I'm doing worse than I did last year. I'm doing better than what they thought . . . this year.

## What the Tech?!

*May 20, 1998*

Somehow, somewhere, my grandmother is laughing. When she was alive, she never took much of a fancy to fancy things. Gadgets, she called them. Nothing more. Try as I might to convince her that I needed the computer or the copier or the fax machine, she'd just shake her head and say something like, "Who needs all that stuff?"

Like answering machines. If you're not home, she'd remind me, whoever's calling can always call back.

I wonder what she would think of this errant Galaxy Four satellite—the one that effectively knocked out almost every fancy-schmancy pager in this country. *Good enough,* she'd probably figure.

Now, God forbid, you have to wait to get back to your office to find out your boss has been scouring the hallway for hours looking for you.

Or that your lawyer can't get back to you right that second on clause two in that oh-so-crucial contract. Maybe now he has to wait to chat with you in person. *There's a thought,* my grandmother would likely snap. Person-to-person contact.

Before e-mail, before voice-mail, before the Internet, before people started acting less like people and more like machines.

We need this stuff, and we like this stuff. But somewhere my grandmother is saying, *we don't have to live and die by this stuff.* After all, it's just stuff.

## Revenge of the Nerds!

### April 1, 1998

You know, despite all our technological advances, I really think the world still hates geeks. And you know the folks I'm talking about. Glasses a little thick. Pants a little too high. Personality a little too lacking. Doesn't matter that geeks often end up very rich; I think we even acknowledge that much.

Still, we figure they're not the football team captains. They're not the presidents of the student council. They're not cool.

Well, let me tell you something. I know geeks. Geeks are friends of mine.

Understand, I have some biases here—I'm kind of a geek myself. But that's another story. What burns me up about this anti-geek rap is how much it misses the point—namely, how often geeks see things before others do.

How confident geeks were that the Internet could be a money-making venture when supposedly cool money types said no way. And how sure were the geeky Web-browser builders that their guides could be revenue builders, too. That you could set up a post on the Web and attract not only users, but also advertisers for those users.

Look at Lycos today, securing thirty million bucks in electronic commerce deals in one day—proof that the 'net can play, if you have the patience and the vision. Geeks have that. Pity that the high school football captain doesn't see it. And probably, sadly, never will.

# CHAPTER 7

# *TAKING ON TAXES*

*Some people tell me I'm a little obsessed with taxes, and that I rant about them too much, almost to the point of shrillness. Perhaps they're right. But I strongly, indeed vehemently, believe that our tax code could be the economic death of us. It's not only because we seem to get so little for what we pay, but because government at all levels assumes we'll keep paying, keep wasting, and keep foisting one worthless program after another on the taxpaying public.*

*Now don't get me wrong. There is much the government does right, but there's a lot the government does wrong. Unfortunately we pay for the whole thing, good and bad. And we do it in a system that punishes those trying to succeed in it, and ultimately attacks the very folks making it possible for all of us to enjoy it.*

*I remember that one reviewer said I sounded like a reverse Robin Hood—praising the rich at the expense of the poor. My point was not so much to honor the rich, but to remember who is paying the bill, and who continues paying the bill. Our progressive tax code has now become the bane of our collective existence. Stating that, railing against that, and constantly reminding viewers of that, is my passion and my mission. For those who tire of my ranting, I remind them of their secret weapon: the remote control. For those ready to hear me out, I remind them of something else: our collective need to act!*

# Kill the Death Tax

### *June 24, 2004*

I want you to picture being dead. In a coffin. Being lowered into the ground. And just as they're ready to put the dirt on you . . . a hand, out of nowhere, reaches into the casket to touch you. Actually, to take something from you.

You can't fight, because—like I said—you're dead. So the hand creeps into your pocket and takes your wallet. Your whole wallet. Just before you're finally put away and done away, away goes whatever you had left in this world.

I'm laying it on to pass on this warning: The government is coming to a casket near you. The death tax that we thought we'd ended is coming back. And the hand of Uncle Sam is coming back, too. Unless Congress acts to stop it, we'll be seeing it in just a few years. The estate tax. We thought we killed it, but it's alive!

Now that the stake in the heart seems to have missed the heart, some liberals couldn't be happier. They figure, *You're dead. You don't need it. The government does. The hell with your family. Or heirs. The hell with Uncle Frank. It's Uncle Sam who wants to rifle through your pockets.*

Never mind that you paid taxes in life. You'll pay them again in death. And you'll pay dearly. On the exact same dough.

I heard a liberal last night say that it's only fair, and that only the rich need bother worrying. Tell that to small business owners or farmers. I don't think they think they're rich. But what will it matter when they're dead? When *we're* dead?

You can't fight in a casket. That's why I thought I'd grab you now before you are in that casket. So now, while you still have blood in your veins, fight some greedy politicians who seem to have ice water in theirs.

Then may you rest in peace.

## Tax Cut to the Chase

*November 12, 2002*

Have you ever heard something so many times that you begin to think it's true?

Take the issue of tax cuts. To hear liberals tell it, the rich get all the breaks. So don't make those cuts permanent. That's the story most networks and newspapers report.

Here's the story they do not report: The top 1 percent of wage earners pay more than 37 percent of the total taxes in this country. The top 5 percent of account for more than 56 percent of all taxes. The top 10 percent? Try 67 percent of all monies raised for Uncle Sam. And the top 25 percent of wage earners? Get this: They account for 84 percent of total taxes collected in this country.

And here's something you probably didn't hear from liberals: Even after the tax cuts are fully phased in, the richest will pay an even greater share of taxes. In other words, they're footing our bill. And they will continue footing our bill.

It'd be like going out to dinner with friends. Your buddy at the table picks up the bill, and some knucklehead has the audacity to say, "Joe, you should have left a bigger tip." Now, some Democrats promoting the class war say, "Good, that's the way it should be. And yeah, Joe, you should have left a bigger tip."

But when you realize that the richest among us are paying for the bounty of the government for us . . . We should at least, now and then, try a thank-you.

# Non$ense!

*January 7, 2002*

When is a tax hike not a tax hike? Apparently, when Washington says it isn't a tax hike.

But let's be clear here. If you're aiming to roll back a tax cut, that's a tax hike. Forgive my provincial view, but throwing out some of the president's tax cuts down the road is just as good as raising 'em.

Why? Because left alone, your taxes should be going down. Changed, they will go up. It's that simple.

So why don't some people see it what way? People like Democratic Party chairman Terry McAuliffe. He tells me it's just revisiting a tax cut that was too big. Who cares? Now, it's the law.

If you change the law, and cut the cut, you'll hike the tax. So let's cut the crap and cut to the chase. Tax cuts promised and given should be tax cuts administered and cleared. I'm naïve enough to think that Congress should stand by what it does. And I'm stupid enough to think they feel the same way.

It's like friends. You stick with 'em because they're worth it. Tax cuts are the same way, Congress. It's like your word. Stick with it . . . because we're worth it.

## $illy!

*May 29, 2003*

So I'm at this big shindig with a largely liberal group of venture capitalists—yes, there are actually quite a few—who decide to gang up on me and my support of this tax cut.

"A blatant sop to the rich," one said.

"Our children will suffer," another railed.

When it was my turn to speak, I said simply, "You guys look like you're doing okay. If you don't want the tax cut, for God's sake, don't *take* the tax cut."

My point is this: If you don't want that tax cut coming your way, send it back. If you don't want the extra bump in your paycheck, send it back. If you don't want more money to do more buying, or more investing, or more saving, send it back. If you think the government's a better place for *our* money, send back *your* money. If you think the government has all the answers, give the government all your dough.

It's too late for you to lecture other people on what they should do with *their* money. Practice what you preach and return *your* money. Quite a few of you are very well off and say you don't need it. Prove it, and send it—all of it—back.

As for the rest of us who think we know more about what to do with our money than you want to re-engineer with our money, I suggest this: Instead of spewing a speech, write a check. I'll even give you the address:

Internal Revenue Service
1111 Constitution Ave. NW
Washington, DC 20224

You think those guys have all the answers? Then give 'em all your money. Pay up. Then for God's sake, shut up.

## Cool It!

*May 8, 2003*

As this great tax debate continues, a question: Why is it that, when states and cities are running budget deficits, they invariably raise taxes? Why is that a given?

From where I report to you now in New York City, it's all the rage. Real estate taxes up 18 percent. Subway fares up 23 percent. Higher fees at hotels and gas stations. Toll bridges and tunnels. On buses. On boats. Seems as if you use it, they tax it.

Now I'm wondering about it. Why?

Don't get me wrong. There are probably a good number of valuable government programs. If you give me a year, I'll come up with a few, I'm sure of it. For now, I think most folks are being bamboozled.

If you asked them to choose between paying more for something and getting less of something, I think you might be surprised by the results.

For example, what if New Yorkers were asked to choose between a 30 percent hike in bus fare and 30 percent fewer buses going their way? I think most would suck it up and say, *Okay, instead of ten buses per hour going to Manhattan from my home, I'm going to have to live with seven.*

When times are tough, you have to take tough measures. But we're taking the wrong tough measures. Most people are prepared, I think, to live with less, rather than paying more for less.

Would it kill government at any level to come up with any original thought? Try asking the people. Give them a choice between the bureaucracy you want and the bureaucracy they can afford.

Some might welcome paying more for your services. But I think you're afraid that most would not. So you're not even giving them the option. Higher taxes aren't always the answer. Sometimes, a little common sense . . . is.

## Liberal Nonsense

### *January 30, 2004*

So I'm at an event yesterday, and I overhear a discussion between two obvious liberals about the tax cuts.

"We didn't need 'em," said one.

"And we've gotten all we can expect out of 'em," said another.

This pushy Irish-Italian anchor had to butt in: "So let me get this straight. This tax cut feel-good-effect is already feeling bad."

"Yes," the one guy replied. "We've shot it all."

"Oh, really?" I pointed out. "The strong retail sales, the incredible consumer confidence number, factories humming again, business hiring again . . . all that is a one-shot freak of nature. Even though this shot's been lasting more than a year!"

"Yes," one of them responded, clearly annoyed. "It's all spent. What's the conservatives' next trick pony?"

"Well," I said. "If this is a trick pony, saddle me up, because history proves it gives ya one hell of a ride."

John Kennedy's tax cuts gave us about a ten-year pop, before taxes were hiked again.

Ronald Reagan's tax cuts launched one of the greatest bull markets in history before many of those taxes were hiked again. And this president's tax cuts have sent the economy soaring. That is, unless and until some other brainiac gets the idea of reversing course and ramming them up again.

In the meantime, ram this!

Look, cutting taxes equals a strong economy. Far from a quick nicotine fix, cutting taxes and keeping them cut makes a huge difference in people's spending patterns, and in their spending plans.

I call it the gift that keeps giving, no matter where you are in the income stream. And many are finding it's still giving as they tally up their tax returns. A full half-year of the tax cut was never factored in to reduced rates last year. That's why most taxpayers will see big refunds this year . . . which will likely contribute to big spending this year and beyond.

Because let me tell you something: When rates are adjusted lower, people set their expectations higher. We spend more. We save more. We do more. It's a pity all we hear from politicians is them just prattling on more.

## Fat Cat Farce!

*November 23, 2001*

Those of you who watch this show regularly know that I'm a fan of tax cuts. I think we all pay too much in taxes.

So it might surprise you to find out I'm very much against a whopper of a tax cut Congress is debating now for corporations.

If some have their way, the corporate minimum tax will soon be gone. I have no problem with that. This law—which demands companies pay a minimum to Uncle Sam—seemed flawed to me from the beginning.

Here's what bugs me. They want to give companies all the money they've paid into this tax . . . ever since it was enacted in 1986.

You heard me right—a retroactive refund back to *1986!* That's a lot of years. And a lot of money. Billions of dollars of money.

Under this absurd plan, IBM would get nearly $1.5 billion in refunds. Ford, a cool $1 billion. General Motors, $833 million. General Electric, nearly $700 million.

It's crazy! And it's not fair. Are you and I given these kind of breaks?

Many of us have been paying this ridiculous alternative minimum tax for years. Why not make that retroactive too?

I'll tell you why not. Because it's stupid. Because good tax policy encourages investments and prudent planning for the future, not admissions of failures in the past. A giveaway, whether justified or not, doesn't do a damn thing.

Let me be clear. The corporate minimum tax was unfair. Eliminate it, then. Set policy right now. Don't try to make up for lost time or dollars. Using that logic, every American would have the right to walk up to his nearest IRS center and demand a refund on his overcharges.

Could you imagine the line for handouts? The descendants of former slaves demanding reparations? Irish, Italian, Polish, and God knows who else's descendants demanding past prejudices be monetarily righted? Life doesn't work that way. Our government shouldn't either.

Get tax cuts going for where we're going, not where we've already been. It's one thing to cry over spilled milk; it's quite another to pay for it after it's already spilled.

## Don't Tax, Do Buy

*February 6, 1997*

If you don't tax it, they will buy it. Such seems to be the theme coming out of scores of retail sales numbers out recently.

The Big Apple is a big example. When Telecheck computed recent weekly national chain-store sales data, it turned out that they'd increased by all of four-tenths of a percent. But in New York City, they'd exploded more than 19 percent . . . the strongest year-over-year sales gain for a district ever. *Ever.*

You know why? Because that was the week New York City was experimenting with a moratorium on the 8 percent sales tax. It worked. And it makes sense: that's like a big sale on whatever you wanted to buy, without any sale at all.

As if Kmart needed a sale—its sales are up 8 percent in the latest month. Federated, up 9.4 percent. Sears, up nearly 6 percent.

A lot of those gains came out of the New York City region. Not all, mind you. But analysts say it explains the unusually strong monthly readings we're getting.

Makes you wonder what things would be like if they waived the taxes for more than a week, or a month, or a year.

## When Viewers React

*March 20, 2001*

Tonight we're still getting an earful over our push for a tax cut. I say it's long overdue, especially now that the Fed clearly isn't inclined to cut interest rates in big bunches. Some of you think I'm long overdue for a kick in the rear, and that the surplus could be put to better uses.

This from Walter Cole, Los Angeles: "I don't think you know jack about the economy or business. If you did, you would be out making money and creating jobs, instead of embarrassing yourself on a lousy network like Fox."

Jeff Crane, Fort Myers Beach, Florida: "You say the surplus is our money, so give it to us. First of all, national debt is our debt. You don't seem to talk about government sending you a bill to pay off our debts."

Here's why, Jeff: I don't trust the government to pay off the debt, even if it promises to do so. Even if it puts the surplus in a lock box and vows never to open that box for any other purpose.

You see, Jeff, I figure the government's a lot like me in a bakeshop. The will is there, but the power is not. It's hard for me to keep my hands off those napoleons. It's hard for Uncle Sam to keep his hands off that cash.

You and many others rightly argue that if the government targeted that extra dough to pay off the debt, all would be right with the world. But how do you know it will?

The track record, much like me in that bakeshop, is very different. Because time and again, Congress has proven that if left with some extra cash, it will more than extra spend. And keep this in mind, Jeff—that's your cash. That's my cash. That's all our cash.

I trust you and me and us a lot more with that money than I trust Uncle Sam with it.

I'm not saying that Congress's intentions aren't good. It's just that the results are almost always bad. I just don't trust Washington to do what it says.

It would be like me saying, "Jeff, all my lunch money is now going toward health snacks . . . fruit and salads, that kind of stuff." And not a penny—not a penny, mind you—to napoleons, or cannoli, or that kind of junk. How long do you think I'd stick to that? I'll save you the trouble: not long.

But here's the difference, Jeff. If I cheat; I have only myself to blame. If the government cheats, we're all to blame. Would you give me a free pass in a bakeshop? Of course not. So don't give Uncle Sam a free pass in *your* shop.

It's one thing for me to get fat on my money. It's quite another for Uncle Sam to get fat . . . on yours.

## On My High Horse!

*January 2, 2001*

You'd think with a New Year and all, I'd have made a resolution to get off my high horse.

Well, hold on, my friends, because I'm riding again. What's got me saddling up is taxes, which are continuing to stay up. It's ridiculous. It's sinful. And it's arrogant.

It's ridiculous because it's our money. It's sinful because many in Washington think it's their money. And it's arrogant because many in Washington refuse to think it was ever anything but their money.

Well here's a news flash: it's not. It's ours. Hands off. Give it back.

Because we all need it. We all deserve it. And right about now, our economy could use it.

Because here's a news flash, Sparky: The economy's slowing. Not quite as much as your limp, legal-laden skulls, but close.

And yet, despite one statistic after another confirming that slowdown, no less than the *New York Times* says it would be foolish for George Bush to get his big tax cut . . . even though we're now reporting big surpluses, now a trillion dollars bigger than we thought only a few months ago!

Let me put this new manna from heaven into some perspective. Uncle Sam's running a projected surplus of five trillion bucks over the next decade. Five trillion bucks that's ours . . . not theirs.

Now do I buy estimates that change on a dime and create lots of dimes? No, I don't. But I'd sooner see those dimes in our pockets than theirs. I'd sooner trust our spending plans than theirs. And I'd sooner trust my Aunt Bette with her money than my Uncle Sam with his.

So when I hear some tax cut opponents go on Sunday talk shows and say that people would just spend that dough, I say, *Go ahead, let 'em spend! Let 'em go to the malls. Let 'em buy the cars. Let 'em treat the kids. Let 'em treat themselves, dammit!*

Hell, if they want to go out and buy fifty velvet Elvis paintings, that's their call, not yours.

After all, Elvis was the King. You're just a thief. And a pompous, arrogant one at that.

## Isn't That Rich?

### October 14, 2003

Isn't it rich, being rich? Joe Lieberman yesterday unveiled a plan to make the rich pay their fair share in taxes. He leads a platoon of Democrats who want to roll back tax cuts for the wealthy.

Believe me, the well-to-do need no lobby. But they do need a fair shake.

I think politicians need to wake up to the people who are paying up. I mean, when is giving 35 percent of your income to the government not doing enough?

When is a group's forking over more in taxes than all other groups combined not helping enough?

Which politicians can honestly look at the top 1 percent in this country, paying more than a third of the taxes in this country, and say they are not being taxed enough?

I'll tell you which politicians . . . clueless and ungrateful ones! It's easy to forget the rich pay more in taxes as a group *after* the president's tax cut than before. It's easy to forget that the rich hire more people, buy more things, and do more things. It's easy to forget that the rich pay more Social Security taxes, state taxes, city taxes, municipality taxes, real estate taxes— more taxes than anyone else in this country . . . put together.

As they should. They earn more. They pay more. I'm okay with that. To politicians who have the nerve to say, "You're not paying your share," I say, *Take a look at the tax tables. Read the charts, you trough-feeding, social-program-pushing pimps.*

The very boondoggles you hold dear are funded by the so-called ingrates you sneer at. Rich people aren't evil people. I've known just as many poor schmucks as I have wealthy ones. Character has no salaried pedigree. Get over the name game, and get to the real blame . . .

You. The ones who want to make government bigger.

Wealthy people aren't the problem. Most weren't born with it. They created it. While you were busy railing, they were busy building. And now they're the ones paying.

## Giving Them the Business

*June 21, 2000*

When is the last time you ever saw a business guy on television treated well? Think hard. Think real hard. Having trouble, aren't you?

I'll tell ya why. Because they aren't treated fairly. Ever! The media hates 'em, vilifies 'em. It's been that way as long as I can remember: J. R. Ewing in *Dallas*. Sinister corporate moguls in James Bond flicks. You name it. They're always selfish, scheming, totally devoid of anything remotely decent. And always an easy target.

Just like the Federal Trade Commission. Apparently at the behest of the White House, these guys are going after big oil for the big run up in gas prices. Al Gore suspects price gouging and collusion. He demands answers!

I demand a little more honesty, and a lot less grandstanding.

It's not the oil companies controlling oil prices. It's OPEC— the same OPEC that's shown enough resolve to ratchet oil prices up nearly three-fold in less than two years. And it's government rules and regulations—the same rules for cleaner gasoline that have made it a lot more expensive, particularly in the Midwest.

And it's taxes. Lots of taxes. As *Investors Business Daily* brilliantly points out, taxes are nearly a third of the per-gallon cost of gasoline. And, I gotta tell ya, it's because of us.

We love to drive. We love to drive far, and we love to drive less-than-fuel-efficient cars.

Now, are oil guys saints? No. Do they sometimes seem slower bringing down gas prices than raising 'em? Yes, sometimes. But you could say the same of banks on interest rates.

My point is this: Let's quit scapegoating, and start thinking. And while we're at it, This is for you, Washington: Let's quit blasting business.

Last time I checked, these guys were hiring the rest of us guys. Hey, they're not all saints. But you ain't exactly Vatican material yourself. So drop the 'tude, open your hearts, and quit the seedy PR campaign.

You might get a kick out of playing politics at the pump. But in the end I think it's you who's the real pain in the . . . gas.

# Pity the CEO?

*June 12, 2000*

It is easy to pick on CEOs these days. Their pay is outlandish by almost any standard. And their longevity is decidedly dicey, at least by recent standards.

So it's easy to make fun of them. Some deserve it. But in my humble opinion, many do not. Especially one CEO, who'd shudder if I gave out his name. So I won't. I caught up with him the other night at a charity event. He goes to 'em all the time. And he gives away a lot of money.

But here's the kicker: When he gives money away to any one of a number of causes—from the Multiple Sclerosis Society to the United Negro College Fund to scores of universities—he insists on one thing.

"Don't mention my name."

I'm serious.

He's given, by my count, at least ten million bucks to just one charity over the years. I did the rough math in my head and added up his other donations, and they're something like $50 million.

Fifty million smackers!

But you won't see any school wing named in this guy's honor. No treatment center bearing his name. No scholarship fund with his initials. He insists on anonymity. And he gets it. He's a rare bird. And a good one. And proof, to me, at least, that just because you're a hotshot CEO doesn't mean you have to act like a hotshot CEO. Or brag to the world, "Hey, I'm a hotshot CEO."

My dad used to say, *Neil, don't let success go to your head.* My mom would add, *Let it stay in your heart.*

I think both of 'em would have liked this CEO. I know scores of people who can't afford good medicine, and many more who, on their own, could never hope of attending college, and they really like this nameless benefactor. They might not know who he is. But someone higher than any of us does. And I'm sure he's saying, "Good show"—mainly because this hotshot CEO isn't doing it for show.

# Hypocrites

*May 31, 2000*

I'm always amazed by people who criticize rich people. As if being rich were evil. And as if their money were any less green. Any less impressive.

News flash: It's not. And they're not. And I'm tired of it. Not because I so happen to love rich people . . . I just hate people who dump on 'em just because they are rich.

Take all this fuss in New Jersey about Jon Corzine. He's the former Goldman Sachs cochair who's running against former governor Jim Florio for the Democratic Senate nod in New Jersey.

Mind you, Jon's estimated to have spent thirty million smackers on this race. That's more than any man or woman has spent on *any* statewide race. *Ever!*

His opponents say old Jon is trying to buy his way into office. I say, so let him! He's not using any taxpayer dough. And we're free to decide whether we like this political spendthrift or not.

But to assume we're too dumb to distinguish between the man and the man's money is as insulting as this argument is old. I'm not taking sides here, but this much I do know: He has a right to spend his own money. And we have a right to decide whether he's worth what he's spent. It's not as if money buys you a seat at the table anyway.

Just ask publisher Steve Forbes, who spent bundles of it in two presidential campaigns. Or entrepreneur Ross Perot, as a third-party candidate in two campaigns as well. Or businessman Michael Huffington on a multimillion-dollar failed bid for the California Senate. Or investor Al Checchi on a similarly expensive and futile effort to become California governor. Voters weighed these guys. And rejected these guys. Not so much for the money they spent, but maybe for the message they conveyed.

So give them, and me, some credit. And shut up about all this money fuss.

I say, let 'em spend their dough. And if they waste it, who cares? As long as it's on their dime, or dimes. And not mine.

## Classless War

*March 27, 2000*

One thing I always get tired of in politics is this class war thing. Pitting the rich against the poor.

Take this raging debate over tax cuts. The argument against them, of course, is that they benefit the rich. Never mind that the rich pay more taxes. Or that the top 1 percent of wage earners in this country account for more than a quarter of all tax revenue collected.

The argument is: they can afford to pay more, and they should. That's why trying to lower the capital gains tax rate is always a Herculean struggle—because it's thought to benefit the one group that needs it the least: those Wall Street fat cats.

Well, here's a news flash. There are a lot more fat cats out there. And they don't all work on Wall Street. And they're not all millionaires.

In a well-written piece in the latest edition of *Barron's*, Fleming Meeks concludes that we're en route to seeing a nation of millionaires. That so many Americans have money invested either directly or indirectly in the markets, through everything from mutual funds to 401K plans, that countless Americans are poised to retire with more than a million bucks . . . and many with a lot more than that. In fact, Meeks points out that nearly fifty million households—roughly half of all those in the United States—are now invested in the stock market.

So Washington, the next time you tinker with raising taxes on the money folks pour into their investments, consider this: It ain't just the rich you're taxing. Many of 'em are your constituents . . . and they're getting sick and tired of you picking their pockets as if they were targets on a shooting range.

In the old days, your coy, class-bating game framed the debate. But people are wising up, and building up. Not only their worth, but their wrath. Tread softly here. The Marie Antoinette let-them-eat-cake thing is getting old. Very old.

# CHAPTER 8

# *DEFICITS*

*Y*ou'd think that, with my unending ranting on taxes I wouldn't much care about deficits. After all, liberals say you can't keep a tight line on budgets if you don't keep a tight rein on taxes. I disagree. There's a mistaken notion that tax cuts equal deficits. That canard has been allowed to go unchallenged in the media for all too long.

We know very well that tax cuts create revenue for the government. It happened that way with Ronald Reagan's huge cuts back in the early 1980s—billions upon billions of dollars of extra dough made its way to Washington. There was nothing magical about this: The more money people and businesses saved in taxes, the more money those people and businesses spent on other things. Not only did this lift sales receipts, but the growing demand for lots of products also lifted hiring rates for the people who make and sell those things. And the more people are working—some twenty million extra jobs during the Reagan years— the more money makes its way to Uncle Sam's coffers.

Indeed, when President George W. Bush decided to cut tax rates in his first term, many economists argued that he made a shallow recession out of what could have been a deep recession or worse.

*But there is a remarkable similarity in both the Reagan and Bush tax cuts. While they both triggered economic turnarounds—and yes, more money for more folks to spend—they both did little to control Congress's inherent love of spending. I've come to discover that Congress, in either party's hands, is incapable of restraining its insatiable appetite to spend what it gets— and then some. Productivity booms and a soaring stock market can offset such bureaucratic overreach (as they did during the Clinton years), but for only so long.*

*So, as I see it, tax cuts aren't the problem. Government spending is. Until we get the latter under control, we are at risk of seeing the former spiral out of control. It's why I argue night after night on my show for simplicity in government, and why I take no political prisoners on this issue, faulting Republicans and Democrats alike for not doing more to control spending. I must be striking a chord when both sides let me know they're ticked off. But I also strike a chord with the people who matter: the folks who elect these spendthrifts in the first place.*

## Attention Deficit Disorder

*May 14, 2003*

So many lies, so little time.

I'm not talking about those idiots over at the *New York Times.* I'm talking about deficits and how they're supposed to be bad. They're all lies.

Lie Number One: They'll lead to higher interest rates. Oh, really? Then why are interest rates now the lowest they've been in more than four decades, and we're running big deficits as we speak?

Lie Number Two: The last big deficits destroyed us. Hmm. That's interesting. I think Ronald Reagan was president back then, and, if I recall, not only did interest rates stay low, but the economy took off. And the stock market more than tripled through one deficit year after another.

Lie Number Three: The bigger the deficits, the less government spending. Oh, if only that were true. The pity is, the government has an uncanny way of spending through tight and flush times alike. On average, programs go up at about a 10 percent clip, year in and year out. Please tell me the last time you got a 10 percent raise. So much for government suffering.

Lie Number Four: The deficit this time is the worst ever. Again, a filthy distortion that misses this real fact. As a percentage of GDP, today's deficit represents less than a third of what it was two decades ago.

And Lie Number Five: Tax cuts take money away from Washington. Oh, if that too were true, I'd welcome it. The sad fact is, the more you give back to the American people, the more money makes its way back to Washington's greedy coffers.

So there you are, you self-serving, spending freaks: Tax cuts are good for you. And deficits aren't necessarily bad for you.

Look at the facts. And look at your lies. Then look in the mirror. Please tell me which of these disturbs you most. I already know.

## Watch Out, Mr. President

*June 1, 2003*

Let me get a bias out of the way, right away. I don't like big government. I don't like a government that coddles me, protects me, and then sends me a big bill. I think Gerald Ford had it right decades ago when he countered Jimmy Carter in a televised debate, insisting that a "government big enough to give you everything you want is a government big enough to take away everything you have."

I used to think Republicans hated big government, too. I'm not so sure now, having heard Republican National Committee chairman Ed Gillespie telling the Manchester *Union Leader* in New Hampshire that "the days of Reaganesque Republican railings against the expansion of federal government are over."

Oh, really? Says who? I, for one, worry about a party that has forgotten its roots in favor of pandering to its special interests. Believe me, it's not easy to advocate smaller government. In our supersize society, we want more . . . we get more.

I say, no more. You can do more for people by giving them less and stimulating them more. It is not the government's job to make people's lives better. That's up to us. That might be tough love, but it's love.

And Republicans used to espouse it; but true to their baser political instincts, it's Republicans who are ignoring it. No program is too much, no prescription drug benefit too costly, no government contract too outrageous in this environment. How the heck did this happen?

Don't get me wrong, I still think the president has his basic priorities right. He wants to keep the nation safe, and that doesn't come cheap. He's quite rightly committed money to the things that matter—a strong national defense and, down the road, an even stronger home security defense. Stuff like that matters because in the end, it isn't the economy, Stupid. It's living, Stupid. Most Americans would rather be living first, then take a crack at living second.

But we can't live well in this country if we keep spending like sailors on a drunken leave. There's only so much dough in the till. And let me be clear . . . it's our till! It's our money! And the president wisely recognized that when he fought for, and won, two big rounds of tax cuts.

The issue for the government then, and the issue for government now, is not how much *it* has, but how much *we* have. Let me tell you something: It is far better that we have more than it has, or things will start to get real screwy. All of a sudden you'll have politicians thinking it's their birthright to pad more and more spending, more programs, more bridges and tunnels, parks and buildings, highways and railways. These are nice things, but they're not vital things, and sometimes you have to make tough choices and decide to pay only for the vital things.

We've lost that sense. We've lost that drive, and it could prove the death of us. Again, let me be clear. Giving Americans their hard-earned money back isn't the problem. Making no adjustments to massive federal spending is.

To me, a leaner government is a better government, and a more efficient government. But when you have Republicans saying they have no problem with a fat government and a less efficient government, count me as being very worried about our government and our nation.

And count me as being very worried when I hear President Bush tell a Labor Day audience that he's looking for a jobs czar, and that declining manufacturing jobs demand a government solution.

They don't. The government can't put people to work. A strong, stable, and unshackled economy can and will. It's not up to Uncle Sam to fend for our interests. It's up to us. Keep him out. Keep us in. And keep our politicians—Republican and Democrat—accountable not for the bacon they bring home, but precisely for the bacon they do not bring home. We'll all be better for it.

# Why I Don't Trust My Uncle Sam

*January 26, 2000*

Before I even get into my commentary tonight, I should 'fess up. I'm going into this with a clear bias. I just don't trust the government. And I really don't trust the government's numbers. If I ran my house like those guys run theirs—well, I wouldn't have a house.

Take all this budget surplus talk. If you haven't heard, the Congressional Budget Office now projects that the government will have a $23 billion surplus this fiscal year . . . plus another 153 billion bucks in extra cash from Social Security.

But that ain't the half of it. Over the next decade, the CBO shows a $4.2 trillion surplus. That's about a trillion more than it calculated just a few months ago.

Wow. Makes you wonder what they'll come up with next month, or next quarter, or next year.

Which has me wondering: Who's running the fiscal freak show?

And it got me thinking. What if I did that? What if I were having problems with a creditor and had the audacity to tell him, "Hang in there, because a year from now I'm gonna be on Easy Street"?

He'd laugh in my face. So why isn't anyone laughing at the government?

Is it just me, or do you wonder about how reliable these numbers are? I can see a billion here, a billion there . . . but a trillion? In just a few months? That's a lot of billions.

What's even crazier is all this rush to spend that newfound dough. Here's a news flash: It ain't there! It's made up! It's a guess! A crapshoot! A hunch! And it changes. A lot.

So before you guys start spending on new programs, or fixing old ones, remember this: You've got a lousy track record. And you've got my money. It's those last two things that really bug me. Not the fact that it's my hard-earned dough, but the fact that your grubby little hands are spending it before I'm even giving it!

But again, that's just me.

## Stick to It, Washington

*February 8, 2000*

Do you try to stick to a budget at home? Most folks do—or try to. They carefully set aside amounts for things like groceries and dining out. The idea is not to spend more than what you take in.

But what happens when you start taking in more than you planned? Do you still stick to that budget? Logic dictates that you should. Reality says you don't. And in Washington, the reality is that they won't, either.

And that has me worried. Because a lot of the big surplus assumptions these guys are hanging their fiscal hats on are based on spending caps that aren't being honored.

It was all part of a deficit-cutting spending plan agreed to years ago. Certain programs' funding would be frozen at a given rate. You couldn't spend a nickel over that rate, plain and simple. Sort of like you and me agreeing to spend no more than 200 bucks a month eating out. Not 201 or 210 . . . 200. No wiggle room.

But now, with all this extra dough coming in, the government's finding a lot of wiggle room, and reasons to climb around these caps.

If the president or Congress feels constrained by spending limits on educational funding, they can call it an emergency appropriation. Or they can blow the caps altogether, which is what they're doing now.

Which is all well and good until you realize that the rosy surplus assumptions we're banking on depend on our keeping those caps in place. Blow the caps, you blow the budget. Blow the budget, you blow all that extra dough. You blow all that extra dough, pretty soon you don't have much dough.

You and I couldn't run our budget that way. But we're letting these guys run theirs that way. Only difference is, these guys are spending our money. Or blowing it, as the case may be.

## CHAPTER 9

# *GREENSPAN OR GREEN-SPIN?*

*I*f people think I over-obsess about issues like taxes, they say I take the editorial cake on the issue of one Alan Greenspan. The Federal Reserve chairman is arguably the most influential financial figure in the world today. He is idolized in the press and lionized on Capitol Hill. Few challenge him. Most just try to ingratiate themselves to him. I have known Mr. Greenspan for many years, way back to his days running his own economic consulting firm called Townsend-Greenspan. Back in those days, I used to schlep over to his offices in downtown New York. He was an economic commentator for PBS Television's Nightly Business Report. I was the New York bureau chief at the time, and arranging these Greenspan tapings was a treat—not only because he was so widely followed, but because he was generally very engaging to be around.

I always remind people that I find Mr. Greenspan to be a towering financial intellect in the world today. He was in the early 1980s when I first began covering him, and he certainly is today. But no public official is infallible, and this one is certainly no exception. (He was no Nostradamus during his days as Gerald Ford's chairman of the Council of Economic Advisers, during his

*"Whip Inflation Now" campaign with those laughable "WIN" buttons.) But as soon as we lose sight of the fact that our elected and appointed leaders can sometimes fail us, we can be lulled into a complacency of coverage that is dangerous for journalists to engage in and even more dangerous for their readers and viewers to partake in.*

*That's why, with no personal animosity intended, I take a more critical look at Mr. Greenspan's record. He's done much well, but he's done many things not nearly so well. I have an obligation to examine the entire Greenspan—including, first off, taking him off the pedestal where the financial and political world has put him . . . to their own detriment.*

## Ignore That Man Behind the Curtain!

### *April 20, 2004*

Interest rates are already moving up. Yet we worry what Alan thinks. Mortgage rates already are inching up. And we fret over what Alan will do. Inflation, we know, is percolating again. Yet we find ourselves obsessing anew over Alan . . . again.

I say, stop it.

Alan Greenspan is a smart guy. But last time I checked, he is still a human guy. He's not Oz. But we treat him like Oz.

Please, I beg you, I beg all of us, look behind that curtain. And come down off that yellow brick road. He's just a man, as flawed as you and me at having economic hunches and making financial bets.

Don't get me wrong. Alan is an honorable and decent fellow, but when it comes to blazing paths, let's just say he isn't a ring-leading fellow. He responds to events. He doesn't determine events.

Take a look at interest rates. Many experts are convinced that Alan and his Federal Reserve buddies are poised to hike them, and maybe soon. I say, who cares? They're moving up regardless of what he or those knuckleheads sitting around that big table do.

Here's the dirty little secret that's getting lost: the Fed doesn't control market interest rates. As the name implies, the market does. And the market long ago determined that with the steady spate of improving economic numbers, it was only a matter of time before inflation would become more of an issue.

I'm not even saying *bad* inflation, just inflation. Prices are going higher, not even a lot higher, but enough to raise eyebrows and concerns. Clearly the markets figured that interest rates at forty-year lows were unsustainable in an economy clearly starting to percolate.

That's not a bad thing, it's a good thing. Our economy is improving. Businesses are starting to see more flexibility in their prices, and clearly OPEC itself has seen flexibility in its market: Just look at gasoline prices!

My point here is not to bash Al, but to point out what's really going on. Let's say the guy does eventually start hiking rates. He isn't leading a trend, he's following it. He's continuing to do what the markets have already been doing for him: recognizing the strength in the economy by pushing up interest rates to reflect that strength.

Remember, Al doesn't determine fixed mortgage rates, the markets do. And fixed mortgage rates are mostly based on something called the ten-year Treasury note. That note has backed up close to half a point in little more than half a month . . . and, again, all without the Fed so much as having a conference call.

Al responds to what *is,* not what will be. He will hike rates. I'm not smart enough to say when, but I am smart enough to say he will. And I'm not basing that on what I think, but on the history I've seen.

Al reacted to an economic slowdown years ago by cutting interest rates too late, just like he reacted to an economic boom by raising them too late. Let's just say that Al likes to wait, to see all the data, to make sure he's not doing something drastic. That's probably good analytical common sense. It's just that it's also conservative and tepid, and cautious—very, very cautious.

I'm not saying that Al isn't a remarkable fellow. I'm sure he is. I'm just convinced he's not *as* remarkable as some have made him out to be. We fret too much over his every word, his every act. And history tells me neither is very bold or awe-inspiring. That doesn't make Al "Oz." That makes us . . . cowardly.

## Al and Santa

*July 20, 2004*

What's the difference between Alan Greenspan and Santa Claus? I'll tell ya: Nothing!

Yet to see all these senators tripping over themselves to praise the guy, you'd think Saint Al *is* Saint Nick. News flash: He's not!

Santa deserves the good press. I don't know about Al.

Santa's generous all the time. Alan's generous only some of the time.

If Santa screws up on a toy order, he makes good. If Alan screws up on a premature rate hike, he still acts like he's doing good.

Santa lives at the North Pole but doesn't mind the cold. Alan lives in Washington and just leaves me cold.

Santa's weapon of choice is a list. He checks it twice. Alan's overdone it in the past, and boy did we pay. The worst you could say about Santa is he just made us *play*.

Santa laughs. Alan never laughs.

Santa's a big guy. I like big guys. Alan's a thin guy. I get nervous around thin guys.

Santa says ho-ho. Alan's always saying no-no.

Santa speaks clearly. Asks, Have you been good? Al never speaks clearly. Asks, Have we been overly accommodative to crosswinds that are at odds with inflationary pressures building globally?

What?!

Not once have I heard Santa talk about headwinds when he's flying. That's all I hear out of Al when he and his gang are hiking.

I can understand sucking up to Santa. For the life of me, I cannot fathom sucking up to Al.

So I have an idea. Bring Santa to the Fed. Ship Al to the North Pole. I'd love to see how Santa deals with bureaucrats. And Al . . . with elves.

## Tony Soprano for Fed Chairman

*May 4, 2004*

What if Tony Soprano ran the Federal Reserve? I suspect it would be a very different Fed.

Maybe it was just gleaning the meaning behind the latest Fed powwow and doublespeak that made me clamor for someone who could really *speak*. Directly. Forcefully. Brutally.

Frankly, I'm sick and tired of playing verbal chicken entrails and tea leaves with everything out of Al and his pals. They look for nuances. I'm looking for clarity.

Al hints at pricing pressures building. Tony would point to your neighborhood gas station and say, "They're infuriating."

Al would say we have to be vigilant. Tony would say, "I have to be honest. . . . If this inflation nonsense keeps up, I'm gonna knock it upside the head."

Al would hint at raising rates. Tony would just raise 'em.

Al would fear alarming the markets if he is too clear. Tony would fear alarming the markets if he is not.

Al would leave you guessing where he stood. Tony would leave no doubts where he stood.

Al likes adjectives and adverbs. Tony doesn't *know* adjectives and adverbs unless they come with an "f" in front of them.

Al likes to be admired. Tony likes to be feared.

Al likes to keep the economy humming by not rocking the boat. Tony keeps it humming precisely because he does rock the boat.

Al favors getting in your head. Tony's more in your face.

Sometimes, I think there's something to be said for *saying* something rather than *hinting* something.

Sometimes I think we could all benefit more from the boss who tells you, "You stink," rather than the boss who says your work is not up to acceptable standards.

Sometimes we need a boss to *be* the boss. I prize the guy more who lets me know where to get off in no uncertain terms than the diplomatic phony who masks his contempt in uncertain language.

Elitists, and probably those afraid of getting bumped off, wouldn't welcome Tony at the Fed because he's kind of direct. I

think half the problems in the world today are created precisely because the guy who's there now is not direct. And it's a
bada-shame!

## Admit It. We're to Blame, Too

*March 7, 2001*

As many of you who regularly watch this show might know, I'm
not a huge fan of Alan Greenspan. I think he raised interest
rates too much last year. And we're paying for it this year. He
should cut more. And fast.

But Alan isn't my big beef right now. We are. All of us. Because Alan isn't the source of our problems. He's just one of our
problems. A slow-moving Congress doesn't help. This namby-
pamby response to a big tax cut certainly hurts.

But those are my opinions. And so is this one: We should all
look in the mirror.

No one demanded that we buy up Internet stocks without a
speck of earnings. We did so willingly.

No one said it was our birthright to assume double- or
even triple-digit returns in the markets. Many of us did so
blindly.

And no one said investing was easy. The market just made
it look that way. So lo and behold, when it turned out investing
wasn't easy, we weren't—and aren't—happy.

We're angry—very angry. And we're looking for someone to
blame. The brokers who touted this new Nirvana . . . the
princess of profits who pushed new paradigms.

They said it. But we bought it. And bought into it.

Maybe they had a convincing argument. But in the end, we pulled the trigger. So we take the blame. You know, I can't blame my neighborhood baker for having the nerve to flaunt tempting cannoli and napoleons in my face. Sure, he wants me to buy 'em and eat 'em. That's his wish. But it's my call. And do I look like a guy who'd disappoint my baker? No. So I'm just as guilty as anyone.

I guess it's easy to be angry and sore. Easier still to play the victim. Easy to blame Greenspan, who *did* screw up. Easier to blame Washington, which failed to measure up. But not so easy to blame us, for failing to wake up.

Let me end by quoting a very wise man, Ricky Ricardo, who rightly demanded: "You got some 'splaining to do!" That's you and me both, friends. And some soul-searching, too, while we're at it.

## Cutting Too Late

### *January 3, 2001*

Well, la-la-di-dah. Interest rates are coming down. So let me cut to the chase. It's about time.

Only one question, Mr. Greenspan. What took you so long? Only three weeks ago, you and your buddies on the Federal Reserve opted not to do diddly on rates. What changed? What happened? What new piece of data did you get?

I'll tell you what you got. An earful. From average folks who were hurting. From businesses that were stumbling. From markets that were free-falling. And from a world, that was asking, "What the heck are you thinking?"

Today's move is a bold move. And the right move. I just don't know if it's enough of a move.

For a year now, I have lamented on this show that interest rates were going up with no evidence that prices were going up. That Mr. Greenspan was chasing a ghost—an inflationary threat that wasn't there. He had no way of predicting the double whammy of soaring energy prices. But I think he should have been prepared to address them. He should have cut much sooner, acted much quicker. He didn't, until today.

It's too early to say whether this half-point cut does the trick. Alone, I don't think it will. But it does send the right message. Namely, that Alan *gets* the message. That from his world of Mount Olympus, he finally sees that average folks are hurting.

The pity is that it took a lot of screaming and suffering to get this move. But what's that they say, "Better late than never?"

No, the crying shame isn't that he didn't act. It's that he didn't act, *until now.*


# When Legends Go Bad

### *October 30, 2000*

Many of you have criticized me, perhaps for good reason, for criticizing Alan Greenspan. My view, often stated here, is that the Federal Reserve chairman has hiked rates too many times.

But as some of you pointed out in cards, letters, and e-mails—who am I to judge the guy truly responsible for the economic times we enjoy today? As I myself once put it, "It's like second-guessing Yoda." I'm not fit to judge. But no matter, I judge anyway.

And now I take some small comfort in knowing some other people, decidedly more accomplished, are worried too. Very worried.

A lot of the CEOs who gathered in Boca Raton, Florida, last week are now citing the same issues I've been blathering on about here: that a soft landing is looking a tad harder than we earlier thought. Growth is slowing. Tech stocks are hemorrhaging. Manufacturers are stumbling.

Now I'm not saying that's all Greenspan's fault. For example, he can't control what happens to energy prices. But my view is that he should have seen it, and cooled it, ahead of time. And he didn't.

But if he didn't appreciate the double-whammy effect on our economy, a lot of these CEOs did . . . and do.

There are CEOs like Sprint's William Esrey, who fret over a devastated stock and similarly devastated employee morale.

Or McGraw-Hill's Terry McGraw, who predicts the problems we dismissed are now coming home to roost.

Or Eli Lilly's Sidney Taurel, who fears the prospect of price controls handicapping his industry's profits.

What worries me is that these guys are reluctant to take on Mr. Greenspan and say outright, "Al, you screwed up."

Legends die hard. Questioning them dies harder still. I'm not saying the guy isn't a genius. And I'm certainly not implying I am. But this much, my friends, I do know: Geniuses do screw up. And if they're human enough to screw up, we should be human enough to speak up. Because the only thing worse than discovering that the emperor has no clothes is not bothering to check out what he's wearing, or not wearing, in the first place!

# CHAPTER 10

# *BOSSES*

*B*ecause I've been doing this business-journalism thing for a quarter century now, I've come to know just about every major prominent chief executive, money manager, politician, senator, congressman, and several U.S. presidents thrown in for good measure. I've examined some very closely, others just in passing, yet all with a reporter's notebook and a quizzical eye.

By now, the numbers are staggering—obviously well into the thousands of money and political types who, at moments, have guided our lives, and sometimes even ruined our lives. I've tried to glean what qualities make for the best leader, and what aspects undo supposedly promising leaders. I've come to discover that they're not the obvious issues you'd think. Their backgrounds and educations seem to matter less than their raw nerve and gut. Some leaders are born that way, others grow that way, the best stay that way.

My favorite part of my job is seeing them, talking to them, getting inside them. It's why I think I have the best job on earth. I get to see how the mighty stay mighty, and how the others do not. I'm no armchair psychologist, and none of my insights will make any Wharton business school discussion, but take them for what *they are—a long-serving journalist's insights into what makes some people succeed, and other people fail.*

## The Smallest Slight, the Biggest Headache

*February 11, 2004*

My father used to say, "Neil, be careful how you treat people on the way up, because you're going to meet them all on the way down."

I never forgot that. His message was as simple as it was true—don't be a jerk. It always comes back to bite you. I suspect that more than a few big corporate honchos have found the wisdom in that warning.

Just ask Martha Stewart. By all indications she not only treated Douglas Faneuil poorly, she treated him horribly. He was the low man on the totem pole, the broker's assistant who got her wrath—and later, her number.

In stinging testimony, Faneuil spoke of Martha Stewart as someone who routinely berated people on the phone, particularly him. Sometimes it concerned substantive issues, more often, silly issues. She'd scream about being put on hold. She'd scream about the music that was playing when she was on hold. She'd scream about the audacity of a brokerage giant to be subjecting big shots like herself to lousy music when she was on hold.

And she'd scream at Faneuil himself for being everything from clueless to incompetent. And something tells me Faneuil tracked it all, recorded it all, and remembered it all. He got his chance to unload to a jury that probably came away less than favorably impressed by the decorating diva—not so much for what she said and did, but for how she said and did it.

I just wonder how differently that testimony would have been had Faneuil been treated more politely by Stewart. What if she was pleasant? What if she laughed with him? Or joked with him? Or kidded him? What if she didn't demand answers, but calmly asked questions?

I guess we'll never know, but I bet that had she been a little kinder, he wouldn't have felt so free to be a little meaner, a little edgier, a little tougher on the stand. It's just me, but I think people who are treated like crap relish dishing out the same stuff when they get the chance.

Who knows that better than Michael Eisner? This past week he got an unexpected and apparently unwelcome takeover bid from cable giant Comcast, and all because he dismissed the originally friendly overtures from the company as silly—maybe even a waste of time.

His reaction was as predictable as his past performance. He treated Roy Disney like an annoying Disney family hanger-on, ignoring his advice and, more often than not, ignoring his questions. Finally Roy walked, and now he's leading a palace revolt that some say precipitated the Comcast bid itself. It's hard to say. This much is easy to say: When you burn enough people over enough time, when you assume you're on top of the world and ignore the rest of the people in the world—well, you have a world of problems.

It's the little things that do it. Ignoring guys who want your ear, and others who seek nothing more than an acknowledgment that they're alive. Few big cheeses act that way. It's why some big cheeses get in big trouble.

Dennis Kozlowski, the former high-flying and high-spending Tyco chief executive, seemed to put more emphasis on fancy art and pricey umbrella stands than he did his own people. He didn't seem to care that he was potentially bankrupting them, only that he was enriching himself.

Martha, Michael, and Dennis have as much in common as I do with Jack LaLanne, Bruce Jenner, and Derek Jeter. But I suspect that what bonds them is the personal behavior that sometimes defines them.

Each in his or her own way isn't exactly gifted with people skills, particularly when it comes to dealing with "little" people, people who can't seem to do much for them.

The reality, of course, is that each person we encounter is part of our circle, whether we acknowledge it or not. My father also used to say that there's no energy wasted in a smile and a kind word. Sometimes they go a long way.

Just like sometimes not doing either can go an even longer way.

Just ask Martha or Michael or Dennis.

## When CEOs Were Great

### October 25, 1996

The greatest test of character, it's been said, is not how we handle success, but how we deal with adversity.

James Burke of Johnson & Johnson will forever be remembered for his forceful, in-your-face handling of the Tylenol tampering crises of the 1980s. Within hours of the first deaths, he took to the airwaves. He promised a worldwide recall of Tylenol products. He opened up twenty-four-hour phone banks for worried consumers. And he spent millions changing the product and its packaging.

It was costly. It was unprecedented. But it worked. Not only did J & J survive the crisis, but Burke became a corporate hero.

Just like Lee Iacocca had done years earlier, rescuing Chrysler from the brink of bankruptcy and whipping up a frenzy of loyalty among workers, investors, and most important, customers.

Fairly or not, the same cannot be said for Jeffrey Erickson, the savvy TWA boss who resigned last night, in the wake of that Flight 800 plane crash and perceptions that he botched the fallout.

Sad, because Mr. Erickson almost single-handedly turned this distraught carrier around. No matter. Neither he nor TWA recovered from those initial images of anguished and angry victims' families, demanding answers or, at the least, support from TWA officials.

Bookings slowed. Troubles mounted. The crash wasn't Erickson's fault, of course. Maybe not even the fallout. But the result was clear. Today Jeffrey Erickson is the former CEO of TWA. Fairly, or not.


# Roger That: A Man and a Mission

### *October 7, 2004*

Bill Clinton was our president. George Bush was still a Texas governor. John Edwards was still a trial lawyer. The Twin Towers still stood. And the nearly three thousand people in them still lived.

October 7, 1996.

The Yankees were en route to winning a world series. The then-reigning champs, the Atlanta Braves, were en route to losing one. CNN was the news network of record. Its biggest competitor, MSNBC, the greatest challenger to that record.

Few noticed on this day eight years ago that yet another news challenger was rising. Fox News seemed like an oxymoron. Many in the media called us morons. Many laughed. Many more dismissed. But Roger Ailes didn't laugh. And Rupert Murdoch didn't dismiss. And my old friends and colleagues at CNBC, who claimed I had entered the witness protection program, soon grew to realize I had entered something a little more.

We had no news infrastructure. No fancy bureaus. Barely any bureaus at all. No state-of-the-art equipment, barely much equipment at all. Our only saving grace was our singular saving philosophy: News . . . fair and balanced. People once laughed at that tagline. Little did they know it would tag quite a line. It would start a revolution among a nation of viewers sick of news being spoon-fed them, and open to a news channel that respected them.

I remember when Roger Ailes asked me how I would present business news differently. I told him I would simply try to do it fairly, reminding viewers that some CEOs are crooks, but not all. That some companies are bad, but not all. That there's much wrong with capitalism, but much more that is right. That I wouldn't act like the smartest kid in the class, mainly because, as Roger reminded me, I *wasn't* the smartest kid in the class. That we biz anchors don't have to be so darn serious or self-important now!

I knew enough to believe that business news needn't be dull. It was then, but I hope people view it differently now. It took a channel like Fox to change people's views. Because it took a channel like Fox to finally respect people's views.

The rest, as they say, is history. Happy anniversary. And thank you for making it possible.

## The Power of Kindness

*November 22, 1999*

Never underestimate the power of a kind word. Time and again, I'm amazed by how a little act of kindness can go a very long way.

Take the industry survey out this week—Thanksgiving week, no less—that reveals the one word workers want to hear is "thanks." Money's nice. A flexible work schedule is nice, too. And a rewarding job, nicer still. But if workers across a variety of industries are right, none of that matters as much as the feeling of being appreciated. As one survey respondent put it, being told, "I matter."

I'll never forget a boss in a prior job, who made a big deal out of Saint Patrick's Day every year. Given that he was 110 percent Irish, it wasn't surprising. Here's what he did for the troops: Every March 17, he'd set out a huge spread of corned beef, cabbage, and Irish soda bread and leave it piping hot all day for every worker to dig into, regardless of their shift, regardless of their status. He didn't have to do it, but he did. It was such a random, but deeply meaningful act of kindness that he inspired enormous loyalty. He was, and is, a very good person. A person who said thank you, and to whom much thanks and hard work were given in return.

That's because there are certain things you can't put a price tag on. Just like the old buddy of mine who joined a hot Internet startup—not so much for the promise of big bucks, which was substantial, but for the camaraderie of the troops, which was even more so.

Reason enough for workers surveyed this Thanksgiving week to say good pay is nice, but a good word nicer, much nicer still.

## Chainsaw Chucked

*June 16, 1998*

Al Dunlap never said he wanted to be loved. Judging from the headlines trumpeting his abrupt firing at Sunbeam, he wouldn't be disappointed.

I've seen 'em all. *Chainsaw Chucked. The Chainsaw Gets the Ax. Sunbeam Chainsaw Massacre.* You get the point. And so did Al, a corporate maverick who lived by the sword, and ultimately died by the sword.

The prince of pink slips gets slipped himself. Trite. Easy. A joke that doesn't even need a punch line. Reason enough that not a single major daily newspaper in this country chose to pass up the opportunity to say this corporate crasher got his comeuppance.

Maybe. And I'm not here to justify his layoffs, his radical restructurings, or his self-bravado. Clearly, as the *Financial Times*'s Richard Lambert writes, the sands had shifted. Sylvester Stallone gave way to Leonardo DiCaprio.

Ironically, it was Mr. Dunlap who set up the expectations. And the compensation that led to his deterioration? In a single word: stock.

Pay the board in stock and the board pays attention to the stock. That's good for the boss when the stock goes up. Not so good when it goes down. As boardroom insider Ralph Ward writes, Dunlap made boards accountable, more results-oriented. And quick. "No one likes to have their house catch on fire," Ward said. "But it's good to find out that your new sprinkler system worked like a charm."

Even if it hosed the very guy who created it.

## "The Donald" Brilliance

### *February 6, 1998*

The rich are different from you and me, because sometimes they're crazier than you and me. I don't think Donald Trump would mind me saying that he's a little crazy. Crazy like a fox. He was given up for financially dead back in 1991 . . . under a heap of debt, and facing a heap of trouble. Trouble was, the Donald wasn't troubled.

Maybe it was his pride. Maybe it was his ego. Maybe it was his determination not to go out with the epitaph, "former real estate kingpin." So he renegotiated his debts, and reassessed his friends. "I remember those who suddenly weren't returning my calls," he told me, "and I remembered those who did. And I never forgot."

It was, in retrospect, crazy to think he could get out of his mess. Crazy to think he could dig out of debt. Crazy to think investors would ever line up again to buy into a piece of Trump. And crazy to think he could roll the dice again in Atlantic City.

Just like it's crazy to think, as the Donald does, that you can sell your casino operations for more than three times what they're fetching now. But turn it around—perhaps it's crazy to think this guy's all that crazy, after all.

## When Someone Throws a Pie in Your Face

*February 4, 1998*

My father used to tell me, "Neil, stay humble. In your case, it'll come in handy." You know, I think he was right, because no matter how big you think you are, there's always something that could bring you down, or at the very least, embarrass you.

Take Bill Gates. He's the world's richest guy. Runs probably one of the world's most envied, most feared companies. Here's a guy who doesn't have to kowtow to anyone. Anywhere. Anytime.

And here he is, just back from his tour-de-force performance with global business and political honchos in Davos, Switzerland. He's being feted, and praised, and revered, and, gosh, worshipped.

Yet just as he's en route to another hotsy-totsy reception—this time, given by the Belgian Flemish community—old Bill gets creamed—literally. A guy throws a pie in his face. Bill did not look happy. Handlers, we're told, were appalled. Onlookers looked on. And old Bill stormed out. Not with egg on his face, but a lot of whipped cream. He was the victim, we're told, of a guy who likes to throw pies at the rich and famous. Simple as that. So in a way, it wasn't Custer's last stand, more like custard pie's last stand . . . and maybe not the last, at that.

# Good Bosses Who Take Bad News

*September 29, 1997*

Bosses like to take credit when things are going well. They don't when things are going badly. It only figures. And for the White House, it's only common sense. After all, we're quick to blame the top guy when things stink. Why not tip our hats when things are hummin'? And why, says this president, wait for us to do that?

As he has with each and every positive economics statistic, Mr. Clinton came out today to brag about the latest data confirming steady growth, steady wages, and no inflation. To be sure, it's all happening under his watch.

Never mind that his critics will say he's been blessed by impeccable timing, by a global workforce that's kept competition for goods tight and wages contained. Or that companies in this environment can make money. Or that with Alan Greenspan at the helm at the Federal Reserve, the prospect for inflation running amok is decidedly less threatening.

CEOs like to boast about big earning news. They rarely credit a declining dollar when sales are good. But they are quick to cite a strong buck when sales are bad. It's natural. It's marketing. It's . . . America.

# CHAPTER 11

# *RESPONSIBILITIES*

*I* remember getting a nasty e-mail from a viewer sometime back who was so personally disgusted by me that the mere tone of his missive stuck with me. (Yes, I am sensitive.) He went on to call me every name in the book, capping his carping critique with this ringer: "And you've got a fat ass, too!"

Since I sit behind a table and never stand up on air, I always wondered how this guy knew I had a fat ass. Perhaps he just assumed. I remember responding, "You're right, I do have a fat ass. But I can always lose weight. You, sir, will always remain an ass. Period."

The exchange got a few chuckles, but my point in jest was very much meant in earnest. I, and I alone, take responsibility for my body. I can go ahead and blame a dear Irish mom who insisted I finish everything on my plate (I did her one better as a kid and opted to finish what was on my siblings' plates as well), but why bother? It's my body, my temple, and I wrecked it all by myself.

I think all too few of us are looking in the mirror these days, preferring to blame others for mistakes that we know all too well we—and we alone—made. I'm the first to want to find a scapegoat, but alas, I'm the last to discover there is none. It's me. It's us. And at this point in history, for the good of both, it's now.

# Chewing the Fat

*November 21, 2002*

All right, this might shock you, but I like McDonald's. You might be equally stunned to hear that I've been there more than a few times. Good food, but pretty fattening food. In short, I know what I'm getting into. But I'm the one getting into it. No one has a gun to my head when I walk in there.

That's why I just shake my head at this latest lawsuit against the Golden Arches, filed on behalf of kids who got fat eating the stuff at McDonald's.

First off, kids, look in the mirror. McDonald's didn't do that to you. You did.

Second, talk to your parents. Where the heck were they when you were stopping there every day? And I guess, in one kid's case, several times a day.

Listen up, kids—and the shysters who represent you: When you eat a lot of food . . . you get a lot of fat.

Now there are some among us—the ones I really hate—who, through tapeworms or some other metabolic miracle, apparently aren't subject to this rule. But most of us are. We have choices in life. The food police and the lawyers who Egg-Mc-Muffin them on can't hide that simple fact. You can't legislate or prosecute your way out of obesity.

I know this is gonna be hard to swallow . . . but you are what you swallow.

So chew on this: The weight of evidence suggests that we bear the responsibility for that extra weight. McDonald's just packs the stuff. We pack it in. If you don't know in this day and age—teenager or no teenager—that a Big Mac ain't a salad, and that French fries ain't French yogurt, then look into a lobotomy, not a lawsuit.

And for God's sake, get real. You're free to do a lot of things in this country. Getting fat is one of them. Suing someone because you do . . . shouldn't be.


# We Are What We Eat

### *November 22, 2002*

This McDonald's thing got me thinking about something grander than the Golden Arches—the government, and what it should and shouldn't do.

My fear is that bit by bit, lawsuit by lawsuit, tax claim by tax claim, the government is taking something away from us every day. Sometimes clearly. Often insidiously. But always, consistently.

It gets bigger and bigger, despite clarion calls to make it smaller and smaller. It makes the decisions many of us are afraid to: It tells us what to eat. It tells us what to drive. It takes our money. It tells us how to spend it. We are given lip service, but we pay the ever-increasing bills for its service.

It means well, but it taxes much. It talks of our interests, but it feeds its interests. It clamors for the rights of all, but it feeds the causes of a few. We expect friendly handouts, but we see greasy palms out. The government tells us it's not our fault, when it is. We tell the government it's the solution, when it is not.

Life is a series of choices. *We* make them. Not the government. Just as we should enjoy the fruits of the good moves we make, we should take the lumps for the bad moves we make. Government shouldn't make jerks whole, or lawyers rich. It should let people think. Make up their own minds. Take their own hits. Enjoy their own successes.

We teach our kids there are no short cuts in life, Yet we have a government that aims to shelter us all from the cold, hard realities . . . *of* life.

# Food for Thought

### *January 29, 2003*

Do you want me heading a commission on proper eating? Or leading a fitness class? Let me save you the trouble: No.

After all, do I look like a guy who should be imparting dietary advice? Again, no. It would be stupid, and it would be hypocritical.

Neither seems to matter much to the United Nations, though. In one of the dumbest stories I have ever heard, Iraq is set to chair a UN conference on disarmament this spring. Iraq. I kid you not.

*World Net Daily* reports that it's actually just part of a alphabetical rotation among the seventy-five member nations. I guess we're closing in on the i's, and Iraq is up for the job beginning May 12. You can't make this stuff up!

A country that's openly flaunting its refusal to disarm is set to chair the commission whose job it is to enforce disarmament. . . . It got me thinking.

Why not have me run the bakeshop, but promise not to eat one cannoli? Or manage the Wendy's and vow not to touch one double cheeseburger? Please—don't even bother.

But the UN apparently sees nothing wrong. *Just part of a rotation,* says one official there. *No big deal.* I'm thinking, Why do we make a big deal out of what the UN says or doesn't say?

Look, I wouldn't dare tell you to put down that fork. Who are these guys saying don't you dare pick up that weapon?

Food for thought.

## Saddam and Cheetos

### September 18, 2002

What if I told you right now, right this minute, that I'm gonna lose twenty pounds? You'd probably be thinking one of two things. One, "I'd go for a lot more than twenty, Cavuto." Or two, "Who's to say you're actually going to do it?"

Bingo. I can say anything I want. Doing it is another matter.

Take this Saddam Hussein weapons inspection news. Everyone's delighted and flabbergasted he's letting those UN guys back in. But the last time I checked, he only *said* he's going to let them back in. Now he has to actually let them in. Then keep them in. Then keep letting them come back in. If this guy's history with UN inspectors is anything like mine with diets, just don't hold your breath.

I have a thing for Cheetos. He has a thing for cheating.

I have a thing for snacks of sweets. He has a thing for sleight of hand.

Here's the difference: I cheat, I have only myself to blame. He cheats, we have only us to blame. I cheat, I get fat. He cheats, we get antsy.

I'd like to take the guy at his word. But just like me and diets, I've learned some people have an easier time eating their words . . . than keeping them.

# What Fair and Balanced Is

*August 7, 2002*

A lot of people have a whole lot of problems with the concept of "fair and balanced journalism." Giving two sides to a story equal weight, equal measure, equal importance.

I know it sounds like I'm bragging about the place I work, but that's what I love about the place where I work. We give you both sides. A bull . . . with a bear. A Republican . . . with a Democrat. An optimist . . . with a pessimist. Some of you read into that what you will. I've been savaged as a right-wing nut. And, just yesterday, as a liberal scumbag who should drop dead. I guess that means I'm doing my job.

But what's more perplexing are the mainstream media guys who like to think this fair and balanced talk is just that: talk. Believe me, it is not. And this notion that it's a cover—or as one journalist put it, "a cloak screen for conservatism"—is ridiculous.

The way I see it, you have two choices today: Get your news with all views or get your news with one view. Get your news reports saying that all CEOs are crooks, or get your news covering the nine or so who are being investigated as crooks, and covering the nine thousand who are not. Get your news reports that say all companies are failing, or get your news reports that more than seven out of ten companies are not. Get your news thinking all stocks stink, or get your news learning that most actually do not. Get your news from a liberal blasting everything corporate, or get your news from that liberal and the corporate guy he's bashing.

Some in the media love to dish it out. Some in the media can't take it. I can live with the slings and arrows. Can the rest of my media colleagues live with themselves?

## What Fair and Balanced Isn't

*August 8, 2002*

Yesterday I talked to you about what I think fair and balanced news is. Here's what it isn't: picking and choosing stories based on an agenda.

Item One: Enron. Lots of stories on ties to the Bush administration, but barely a mention that former Clinton Treasury secretary Bob Rubin lobbied heavily on behalf of the company.

Item Two: Global Crossing. Big corporate shenanigans there, maybe even bigger than Enron, but nothing. Nada. Zip. Maybe because Democratic Party chairman Terry McAuliffe made a cool $16 million off it?

Item Three: The Bush economic team. Lots of press all but calling 'em boobs at the switch. But nary a word about how these boobs managed to cobble together a rescue package for Brazil when no one thought they could.

Item Four: The economy. Stories everywhere about how we're going to hell in a hand basket, even when economic news says clearly that we aren't.

Item Five: Iraq. Wow. All I'm seeing is how attacking 'em is going to be the undoing of the world and us. But wait a minute—didn't they say the same thing a decade ago, giving people the willies, without giving them the facts?

I'm not here to take sides, just to take issue. And I'm not here to condone Republican sins any more than I'm here to cover Democratic ones. I say, cover them all. Report them all. Give viewers and readers all.

I've actually heard from a journalism professor who says that this Fox approach makes him ill. No offense, Professor, but you make me sick. You say we corrupt news. I say you corrupt students. After all, if viewers don't like me, they can always turn me off. You don't come with a remote, Professor, so your students aren't so lucky. Pity.


## All Things Considered, a Nice World

*February 26, 2003*

One more word about "fair and balanced."

A lot of people say I'm a bit too upbeat when it comes to the economy, maybe even life in general. I'll freely admit I'm a glass-half-full kind of guy. That doesn't mean I don't and won't report the bad news. What it does mean is that I'll sure as heck give you the good news, too. That's what fair and balanced financial news means to me.

And today, I'd like to commend *USA Today* for doing the same thing. In a great cover story in its financial section, the newspaper balances out the half-full and half-empty arguments on how we're doing. I loved it. Because, while citing things like declining stock prices and soaring energy prices, the newspaper also reported declining interest rates and soaring home values. The bad news *and* the good news.

That's all I'm trying to do here. My beef with most of my colleagues is that more than a few of them love to accentuate the negative and forget about the positive. There are good things going on in this economy. And, just as the president mentioned yesterday in that meeting I attended with fellow economic geeks, he's an optimist about where we're headed. So am I.

Not everything's perfect. But clearly not everything's bad. We try to offer that perspective in broadcasting. I was delighted to see *USA Today* doing the same thing . . . in print.

Who says I'm not contagious?

# CHAPTER 12

# WHAT ABOUT BILL? PONDERING THE MAN FROM ARKANSAS

*I* remember one historian referring to Bill Clinton as the political enigma of our times. I liked that description because I think it fits a man who was arguably among the smartest presidents we have ever had. I recalled his long-shot candidacy back in 1992, and how he repeatedly came back from otherwise assuredly devastating revelations, financial and personal. Any one of the scandals he encountered—some set by him, others set by those eager to undo him—would have brought down other men. But not Bill Clinton.

His critics do him a huge disservice with their incessant "Bubba" and Monica Lewinsky jokes. They try to trivialize his essence, and miss his bigger message. It's a message both Democrats and Republicans would be wise to understand, maybe even emulate. That's because Clinton had a knack for understanding the times and seizing the moment. He moved deftly to the right after his party was blown apart in the 1994 midterm elections, and safely ensconced himself in the middle when the opposition took on a zealous, right-wing tone during his impeachment in the House of Representatives.

*He survived those who wanted to do him in because he had a knack for doing them one better. They hated him for it. But I gotta tell you, as a journalist, I marveled watching it, and him. I've seen his charm up close, in interviews, including my own at Fox, and in his candidate days when I was at CNBC.*

*Some call that political expediency. I call it just being politically smart. There are dangers in such a strategy, however. Some critics say it can lead you to avoid taking important risks. Others say it can lead you to take too many risks. Regardless, I will always look back at the Clinton years as economically sound ones, but ultimately safe ones, where an administration blessed by a confluence of favorable conditions refused to condition the country for something higher, better, maybe even riskier.*

*I guess we'll never know. Of Bill Clinton, this much I do know: He is one of a kind.*

## In a Conundrum over Clinton

*January 19, 1998*

Would you let Bill Clinton watch your kids? Well, I guess that depends on whether or not the kids were teenage girls. But without being flippant, I remember one poll asking that very question of some Americans. The overwhelming response was . . . Hell no!

But we have no trouble with the guy running the country. It's the paradox that's been plaguing Bill Clinton ever since he came into office. Morally, we judge him poorly. Professionally, we think he kicks butt. And that's what makes damning the guy—on the very night he tells us about the state of our union—so daunting.

Most of us are feeling good. But here's why we're feeling good: Unemployment is at its lowest level in more than forty years. Mortgage rates are at their lowest level in more than thirty years. And inflation—what inflation?—was at 1.6 percent for all of last year. You'd have to go back to John Kennedy's Washington days to see things this good.

And the coup de grace? The government's taking in more money than it's spending. And oh yeah, gasoline's about a buck a gallon. Beat that!

I guess you could say we've compartmentalized as much as the president reportedly has. No, we don't love the guy. But boy, we love this economy. And for now, fairly or not, nothing else seems to matter.

## Not So Impeachable Economy

*January 5, 1998*

Here we go again. Senate Majority Leader Trent Lott has set Thursday as the day to take up the issue of impeaching the president of the United States.

If the markets were shaking at his words today, they didn't show it. And that's the remarkable thing about this whole impeachment mess. The uglier it gets, the prettier stocks look. Not all stocks, mind you. And not all the time. But enough of the time to convince even diehard bears that if anything is to bring down the market, it won't be this. Not yet, anyway.

Which gets me back to my real point here: At what point does all this impeachment stuff make a point? When witnesses are called? When it drags out? When the certainty of not impeaching the president begins to look uncertain?

Hard to say. But something tells me Wall Street has been merrily roaring along, convinced this wasn't going anywhere, convinced that participants in this country and other countries felt that way, too.

It's worth noting that during the time of our first presidential impeachment, back in 1868, the economy was humming, too. Attention was focused more on the good times outside Washington than on the sinister implications inside Washington. That's why America barely noticed that Andrew Johnson's impeachment fate was saved by just one vote.

We'll see if history repeats itself.

## Markets Hoping the Best for the Man from Hope

### *December 16, 1998*

What if we've got it all wrong? What if the markets really don't give a rat's pa-toot about this impeachment stuff, or even this Iraq stuff? Try as we might to hype its urgency, maybe, just maybe, there's no urgency at all among these stock market guys.

My friend Yale Hirsch, the market historian, likes to remind me that markets do indeed rise and fall on a series of events—but that over time, the market develops its own tempo, its own psychology, dictated by unique, day-to-day events.

Talk to any stock expert and he or she will tell you that the market abhors uncertainty. But seeing as life itself is uncertain, I'm not even sure I buy that one.

No matter. The prevailing wisdom is that, since we don't know where this whole impeachment thing is going, or how a potential invasion of Iraq could change that, we wonder—and wonder nervously, at that.

But sometimes things don't turn out the way we think. Experts thought that stocks would tank when we invaded Iraq back in 1990; they rose. They thought that stocks would soar after Richard Nixon left office in 1974; they fell. Experts thought the market in general would suffer under Bill Clinton; it didn't. Which is my typically long-winded way of saying that, obsess as we must on the day-to-day, someday the market will be wrong.

## A Republican's Democrat

*December 12, 1998*

I don't know about you, but I think the stock market's worried about this impeachment mess. In little more than three weeks, the Dow has stumbled more than 600 points from its record. That's more than 7 percent.

There are a lot of reasons for that, of course. I'm sure many investors are simply cashing in their profits. It is holiday time, after all, and you gotta spend some money, even newfound money. I'm also sure a lot of this recent fall-off has to do with companies like Procter and Gamble and Coca-Cola bracing investors for potentially tougher times ahead. All are factors. All could explain, at least in part, why the market's suddenly in the funk it's in.

But is it me, or have you noticed that a lot of this sell-off dovetails pretty nicely with these impeachment hearings going on in the House?

Tick by tick, gavel-banging by gavel-banging, the market has slid as this whole process has heated up. And now, lo and behold, we're on the verge of seeing the house tell the president of the United States to get out.

We're not there yet. And even then, we're a long way from a two-thirds vote in the Senate, but the fact that we're even here at all says something about Wall Street suddenly thinking the once-unthinkable.

## Not a Starr in Their Sky

*November 20, 1998*

Why is Washington obsessed with Ken Starr but not Wall Street? Maybe because Wall Street doesn't care, and maybe because Wall Street doesn't *want* to care.

After all, if you're a broker or a player in this hot financial marketplace, you perish the thought of anyone raining on it. These are heady days for Wall Street. Major market averages are within spitting distance of records again. Individual investors are buying again. Suddenly global markets are picking up again. And along comes old Ken Starr to talk impeachment again. Wall Street thinks, "Ken, not again."

It's not that these guys are huge fans of the president—the vast majority in this admittedly Republican bastion are not.

But they like what they've seen. A Democratic president. A Republican Congress. And a bull market.

Sure, it looked shaky for a while. But it's not shaky now. And that's why these guys are happy again, convinced that nothing can derail the buying train . . . except, maybe, a Ken Starr who has something new on the president.

But so far it doesn't look like he does, which suits the bulls just fine. That's not to say these guys don't like Ken or even admire Ken. They just have a message for Ken: be a Ken doll, please, and go away.

# CHAPTER 13

# TAKING ISSUES . . . WITH THE DAY

*T*he one great thing about my job is that it's new every day. That's the essence of news, of course, but it's also part of its greatest challenge. News needs context. News needs meaning. News needs analysis.

I think my friend Sean Hannity does a remarkable job every day translating events into everyday speak, so he can lay out the essence of the debate. You don't have to always agree with him (and many on the left rarely do), but you cannot deny that Sean has that rare knack for giving passion to everyday occurrences.

Bill O'Reilly does much the same. His hugely successful program has hit a national chord, not because he regurgitates the news, but precisely because he invariably finds the heat in it, the controversy in it, and yes, the debate in it.

I try, to a much lesser degree, to frame economic issues in a similar way. Sometimes they are the stuff of headlines that jump out at you. More often, they don't readily seem to have much to do with you. Until I provide context. Until I provide analysis. And yes, until I provide my own heat—even if it's a little different from Sean's or Bill's!

# Social Security

*March 3, 2005*

When is something a crisis to you? A crisis could be when your mortgage or rent payment is due and you don't have the money. That's a crisis.

Or you're in school, and you've put off doing a big term paper that's due the next day. That's a crisis, too.

I think we call something a crisis when we don't have a lot of time to deal with it. The less time we have, the bigger the crisis it seems.

Human beings generally don't respond well until we've got a crisis. We finally address the collapsed roof after years of leaky ceilings. We stay up all night to finish that big paper when it could have been easily crafted over the weeks it was first assigned.

My point is, we shouldn't have to wait for something to blow up in our face to fix our problems. Social Security is a problem. I know it gets me in trouble when I say this, but I'll keep saying it. The system is in crisis—just not in the way we're used to seeing it. It's not a tomorrow thing, or even a next-couple-of-years thing But it's a ticking time bomb thing. It's a crisis I'd rather see us fix now, before we all end up in a fix later.

Opponents of reform insist that there's no crisis, no problem. Lots of time to fix it later, so don't fix it now. I think term papers done at the last minute make for lousy term papers. I think fixing broken roofs after they collapse makes for pricier repairs. And I think holding off on fixing Social Security makes for pricier fixes later on.

Look, we know Social Security is running out of money. We know young people are getting shafted. We know that fewer people paying in while more people are getting paid out doesn't add up to a sound system. But we merrily march on. As convinced as Scarlett O'Hara was that it's better to think about all this wretched stuff . . . tomorrow.

The only difference is that Scarlett didn't literally mean *tomorrow*. She was way too smart for that. Are we?

## In Pursuit of Eliot Spitzer

*February 1, 2005*

Since Eliot Spitzer won't talk to me, let me talk to him. So, Mr. Attorney General: Why not Fox? Why not me?

Perhaps because you assume I'll be tough. You're right. But I'd be fair. Some other Democrats were okay with fair. Democrats like Mario Cuomo. He had no problem coming on my show. Or Robert F. Kennedy, Jr. He keeps coming on my show. And Democratic fund-raiser and moneyman Gregg Hymowitz is a regular part of my show.

Your Democratic counterpart in Connecticut, Rich Blumenthal, has been on dozens of times. So has another AG— California's Bill Lockyer. Dick Gephardt was here plenty of times. So was Tom Daschle. And a pretty liberal guy you might know: Howard Dean.

Oh yeah, John Kerry showed up too.

And last, but by no means least, Bill Clinton came when he was president. As president. On this show.

Democrats all. I didn't bite them, or abuse them. I was gracious but fair and tough with all of them. As I would be with you.

But you clearly see things differently. Over the years we've tried dozens upon dozens of times to get you on this show. You're free to blow us off. But I don't think you're free to play games.

You have a tough time mustering the very forthrightness you demand from the people you assail. I think you're very good at dishing it out, Mr. Spitzer. But you seem to have a devil of a time taking it. And now you want to be governor.

Perhaps you figure you can pick and choose your fawning interviews to that office. I don't think New Yorkers are that gullible. Or that stupid. They deserve more.

I have no doubt you can handle tough questions. All I'm saying is, for once, let someone ask them.

## Still in Pursuit of Spitzer

### *February 4, 2005*

You might have surmised that I generally don't have much fondness for people who play games. I'll never forget the CEO of a major company who told me to my face, "I don't come on your show because, dammit, I detest your show and your network."

I was jarred. But I was impressed that he said it to my face. He didn't rely on others to hint at it behind my back. I doubly admire those who take the heat. And one of the best at that was Lee Iacocca.

I could be wrong, but I don't think that guy ever dodged a tough interview. Or a tough interviewer. As he told me one time after a somewhat heated exchange, "If I don't set the agenda, someone else will."

I remember at Chrysler annual meetings, he was big on making sure unruly investors were heard, including corporate gadflies like Evelyn Y. Davis, who at the very least, made such gatherings entertaining.

I think the best CEOs and politicians are those who are tested on the stump, at the stump.

When Iacocca was dealing with quality issues in Chrysler's vaunted K-car line, he freely admitted that the company had a long way to go to closing the quality gap with the Japanese. But he promised he would. And he did.

No question was out of bounds. No issue off the table. Even old ones, like his career implosion at Ford. I'd mention it, and he'd make mincemeat of it.

He was one of the few CEOs I recall who never set ground rules in interviews. And that made for some incredible interviews. He was that comfortable in his facts, and even more so, in his skin.

No wonder Democrats turned to him in 1984 to see if he'd be interested in running for president. He wasn't.

"I don't think I'd be a good politician," he once told me.

He was right. Not because he wasn't honest and direct. But precisely . . . because he was.

# JFK

### November 21, 2003

It was one of those small things that usually goes unnoticed in television news coverage. A new network (not my own) teased two upcoming stories. I'm not quoting it exactly, but it went something like, "A look back on JFK, then took a look forward to Michael Jackson." Two compelling issues joined at the electronic hip. I half expected the next tease to read, "From the King of Pop to the guy who got popped. Next!"

Oh, how far we've come. This past week we've been soulful and soulless at the same time—remembering a president we once thought did nothing wrong, and relishing the bizarre personal life of an entertainer we're convinced did nothing right.

I don't remember much about John Kennedy. I was only five years old when he was killed. I do remember my mother crying for days. She loved JFK. Given her Irish descent, it was as if one of her own had been lost.

I'm grateful in a way that she left this world before all the nasty allegations came out. Before the reports of womanizing and pill popping. I don't know how she would have handled it, or whether she even would have believed it. There's a marked departure from the way we covered things then to the way we cover them now.

Yet I am convinced that, without deconstructing Kennedy, we never would have gotten to the point where we're so zealously going after Jackson. One fed the other. One led to the other. One, in a sense, brought closure to the other.

I suspect that there was something of a catharsis for the American press when the JFK allegations went from gossip among a few reporters to unmentionable musings in a few newspapers. The more titillating, the more we wanted to be titillated. It was like driving past a car wreck. You resent everyone slowing down and stalling traffic to take a peek, but find yourself doing the same exact thing when you drive by.

So it was with JFK. So it is with Michael Jackson. One mesmerizes us, despite all the foibles, while the other captivates us precisely because of those foibles. Each is fair game today. Each is zealously pursued today. Each is put in perspective today.

I'm not here to weigh the pros and cons of such treatment. I'm only here to say it this: Get used to it. As my colleagues in the press are quick to point out, today everything is news. A politician's positions and his peccadilloes. A musician's songs and his sex life. And the creepier, the better. We can argue whether they are all newsworthy. But we cannot argue today over whether or not they are news. They are.

I'm told by some seasoned reporters who covered JFK at the time that they knew of his dalliances; some even knew of his chronic pain. But that kind of stuff didn't make news. Never mind that the behavior was sullied and sinful. We needn't compound the sins by reporting them. So we did not.

Much was rumored and suspected of Judy Garland's drinking at the time, or of Marilyn Monroe's moodiness, but only among a few. Now politicians and their flaws, and celebrities and their sins, are reported with the same zeal and the same gusto.

And it all started with JFK—first with his death, then with the inexorable hunt to deconstruct his life. My father used to say that it would only have been a matter of time before Kennedy's womanizing would catch up with him; that his dalliances with mob mistresses couldn't remain hidden forever; that had he lived, the press would have all it eventually needed to pounce.

It took Vietnam and Watergate to complete the cynical trajectory to rightly question those who misled us and pounce on even those who did not. No president was too grand, no actor or singer too talented, that something couldn't be dug up to mangle the myth.

It's why presidents who soar in popularity come down to earth, and why superstars who seem to own the press are eventually torpedoed by the them.

Like I said, it's a weird trajectory, and its timeline an even weirder one.

But it's why we wasted little time burying a president's perfect sheen only a few years after we buried him, and why we do the same to politicians and celebrities alike before we bury them.

## Corporate Scandals

*July 9, 2002*

You want to know how you stop corporate abuse? Stop lying.

You want to know how you stop corporate greed? Stop stealing.

And you want to know how you stop rubber-stamp corporate boards from pillaging their companies? Stop them from rubber-stamping.

I know it sounds incredibly simple, but behind all this talk of commissions, and rules and regulations, and oversight and hindsight, is this simple commandment: Don't be a jerk.

How difficult is this?

Don't be a crook. And don't act like one. I mean, this isn't rocket science, we can police people better. But that doesn't make them better people. We have to teach ethics first, business principles second.

It's sad but true.

These abuses are the byproduct of a culture that said you could do anything you wanted and get away with it. A culture that admired the ingenuity of a guy who could parse what the meaning of "is" is, but not what the meaning of life is.

I say this: Life is short. Go long. Wall Street is fleeting. Main Street is not.

So to corporate America, let me say this: Try not to impress your *broker* friends, but your *true* friends.

And to the financial community, I say this: Remember who butters your bread—the very slobs some of you chose to ignore. Us.

We can't make you behave. But for those of you who don't, we *can* make you go to jail.

Far more of you are more decent than deceitful, more hard-working than hard-nosed. I want the quiet ones to speak up, and show the bums up. It needn't take a good commission to do that. All it takes is a good heart.

Beginning . . . now.

# Trade

*September 26, 1997*

Have you ever had words with somebody—I don't know, a friend, a spouse, an acquaintance—and all of a sudden, it mushrooms?

Well, don't look now, but it's happening between Tokyo and Washington.

Uncle Sam's slapping some hefty tariffs and fines on some Japanese supercomputers making their way to these shores.

The reason? Well, U.S. supercomputer maker Cray Research says those systems are way underpriced, that they're effectively being dumped here at fire sale prices.

Cray says that companies like NEC and Fujitsu are selling the machines for a lot less than they're making 'em. About one quarter of what it's costing NEC to make 'em, for example. That's why the United States is throwing a 450 percent tariff on that company's goods coming here. But it gets worse, NEC claims it's an outrage and plans to protest to the highest authorities.

It's already gotten the attention of the Japanese government, which is reportedly concerned that this whole thing is getting out of hand.

And now people fear a trade tit-for-tat: You slap fines on us, we'll slap fines on you.

This is how trade wars start.

And you thought things were bad if you and your spouse were going to bed without talking.

# CHAPTER 14

## *ADVICE*

*M*aybe owing to the days back when I aspired to join the priesthood, I love to seek counsel and—wouldn't you know it—I love to counsel others. My dad used to say it was because I never knew when to shut up. He was probably right. But with the added experience of having undergone two life-threatening illnesses, I've gained an appreciation for not only the fragility of life, but also the simple humor of life. That's why I take delight in exploring both on my show and in my columns—to reach outside the proverbial box. I know it sounds clichéd, but I put great stock in simply taking stock. I do it a lot with stories. I try to do it also with humor. And I always try to do it . . . with meaning.

## Tips for Empty Nesters

*August 25, 2003*

This is proving one of the most difficult weeks of my life. It has nothing to do with anything I've done, but what my daughter has done. Somehow she has found a way to grow up in an instant. This little girl who I used to hold by the hand and walk to the park is now walking out on me. She's going to college. She's leaving me.

Don't give me that line she has to spread her wings. It just spreads my depression. And don't tell me it's all for the good. For me right now, it's all bad . . . very bad.

But I know a few things that I should and shouldn't do as I prepare to drop her off at college this week. Consider these free tips for any of you going through similar experiences:

**Tip 1.**   Tell your child you're happy for her, but realize that this has got to be the most horrible day of your life.

**Tip 2.**   Do not overjudge his or her roommate. Multiple rings in the nose, and God knows where else, are just as likely to be innocent fashion statements as they are clear and present signs of danger.

**Tip 3.**   Wear sunglasses. It makes you look cool and your child confident that if you are going to be a blubbering mess, at least you won't look like one.

**Tip 4.**   Avoid baby talk. You might be tempted to say, "Well, buttercup, I think I've packed all your stuffed animals," but just suffice it to point out, "All your forty-eight boxes of God-knows-what are in your room, and there's no way in hell it'll all fit." Sound tough. Talk tough. Think mush.

**Tip 5.**   Don't say as you leave, "Daddy's gonna miss you." Just leave and go. Do not turn around.

**Tip 6.**   Once in the car on the way home, do not converse with your spouse. My wife is taking this even harder than I am, but she has a remarkable stiff upper lip. For all you dads, do not—and I repeat, do not—make it look like we are actually the weaker sex. (We are, by the way.)

**Tip 7.**  Avoid the temptation to phone your child as you're leaving the parking lot. It causes him or her great angst, and even greater embarrassment.

**Tip 8.**  Avoid the temptation to phone your child fifteen minutes after leaving the parking lot. Refer to Tip 7.

**Tip 9.**  Return to life the next day focusing on things like work (and the child who's hundreds of miles away from you), the house (and the child who only moments ago was learning how to walk on the floors of that house), and the neighbors (and the child who only yesterday was playing with their kids, who have left their moms and dads in a similar pickle).

**Tip 10.** Act mature, at least in public. Do anything you damn well please in private. It's your life, after all. And leave it to your own flesh and blood to destroy it.

Now, some might think me selfish and immature for turning on my own daughter. They're wrong. She started it—by growing up!

It's amazing. I'm a business journalist who handles money issues every day. There's something comforting about this emotionless world of money. It's a great refuge from such an emotional week.

Other parents tell me it's the circle of life—easy for them to say. And now my wife and I are forced to contemplate an empty bedroom and even emptier hearts. We're proud we brought her to this day. But why, oh, why did she have to bring us to this day . . . at all?

# Please Don't "Snap To"

*October 11, 2004*

Those of you who are going to make it big out there, and those of who who've already made it big, promise me: Don't snap your fingers at anyone.

I mention this because I was on a plane this weekend, and this one guy—sorry to say I don't know who the heck he was— well, he started acting like he was a really big deal. Barked orders to an aide sitting across from him. And barked orders to the flight attendant as well. But he punctuated those barks with snaps of his fingers.

He snapped for some papers from the aide. Snapped for a glass of wine from the flight attendant.

I don't like snappers. Snappers strike me as rude people. And I don't much like rude people either.

But this guy's aide on the plane seemed to endure it. And the flight attendant seemed to tolerate it. And most of the passengers around this knucklehead didn't seem bothered by it.

I wonder if he could have just as easily made his point without snapping his point. I betcha he wouldn't snap at his boss. No—snappers snap down, never up.

I suspect that snappers are small-minded bullies, who choose to bellow below but cringe above. Once a snapper, always a snapper. Once a jerk, always a jerk.

I think that, in time, non-snapping people will figure out snapping people. And the snappers will snap out of the scene . . . just like that!

I felt like warning this snapper of his inevitable fate. But two glasses into some wine myself, I forgot. And then the flight attendant herself said, without snapping, that I could go ahead and have a third.

# A Tough Pill to Swallow

*December 7, 2004*

So now they've come up with a pill that makes you thin. Or at least won't make you hungry.

It's all the buzz right now: a simple little pill that tricks your body into thinking it's not ravenous for Yodels.

Frankly, I find that very hard to believe.

But docs swear by it. Just like we can take a pill to lower our cholesterol or a certain blue pill to raise something else. It only stands to reason that we can attack the obesity problem in this country the same way.

No offense, but I ain't buying it. Sadly, I've discovered that there are no short cuts in life. The trouble with us humans is we're always trying to find 'em. We play the lotto to get rich quick. Or try a high-protein diet to lose weight quick.

Some do win the lotto. And some do drop a lotto pounds. But very few.

My fear is that we'll all come to rely on a pill to make up for our lack of guts. Among other things, we're losing our guts to exercise more and to eating less—the real cures for obesity in this country. To make it worse, science now offers hope for the lazy—myself included—that we can literally have our Yodels and eat them, too.

Now if only they could find a pill to shrink large craniums. Then we'd be talking.

## Hey Big Spender—Cool It!

*March 4, 2003*

I know this sounds a little impolitic, but I want to offer tips to CEOs who are coming into a lot of money, legally or not, and are contemplating spending it:

**Tip 1.** Don't draw attention to yourself. WorldCom CFO Scott Sullivan was just asking for it by building that $15 million mansion in Florida. The natural question people ask is, "Hey, this is a telephone executive building this place, right? And he's not even the boss?!"

**Tip 2.** Don't act bitchy. Fair or not, Martha Stewart, that's just how you came across. So when things looked bad for you, your reputation sank faster than one of your burned bundt cakes.

**Tip 3.** Don't show off by buying fancy artwork. It's so nouveau riche, anyway. If you didn't have culture before, it's a little late to buy it now. Try pouring the money into Yodels.

**Tip 4.**  . . . which kind of goes with Tip 3. If you do insist on buying artwork, for God's sake, pay the damn taxes on it. Tyco's former bigwig Dennis Kozlowski didn't, anneither did ImClone's Sam Waksal . . . and lwhere it got them!

**Tip 5.**  Don't hire a PR person. If you can't speak the truth yourself, you're admitting as much by hiring someone to create it for you. You're screwed either way.

**Tip 6.**  Don't show up for your big day in court in a big, old, fancy limo. Take a Jeep. Better yet, take a cab.

The point, my little robber-baron friends, is that you don't want to look like a robber and you don't want to sound like a baron.

Image counts for a lot. Money can buy you lots of things. Trouble shouldn't be one of them.

## Why Low Rates Are Like Cannoli

*June 25, 2003*

I've said it before. I'll say it again. Don't leave me alone in a bakeshop. It's way too tempting. I mean, it's as if those éclairs are just sitting there for the taking. Too easy. Too dangerous.

I kind of feel the same way about interest rates. They're almost too low. And too tempting.

For a lot of people, especially people who are in debt, that's good. It keeps their borrowing costs down, and their heads above water. Just some advice: Don't overdo it. Because low rates are like napoleons—great to look at, but you can't just don't go to town on 'em.

Here's why. They're like giving crack to an addict. Don't get me wrong. Most people borrow sensibly and wisely. They don't get in over their head. But some do. And lenders make it almost too easy. And so do very low rates.

People can afford to buy more. And they do. They can leverage more. And they do. They can risk more. And they do.

Right now, that's been okay because rates keep going lower, and the values of homes keeps going higher.

It's sort of like a one-two, croissant-cream puff combo that keeps those with a fix from getting in a fix. But cream puffs do have calories. And interest rates do go up.

Borrowing is cheap and easy today. But that doesn't mean it can't be painful tomorrow.

You go crazy in the bakeshop, you'll pay for it long after you've left the bakeshop. You go crazy with all that easy money, you'll pay for it long after it's not such easy money.

The only difference between tantalizing sweets and tantalizing rates is that the tantalizing sweets just leave you fat. The tantalizing rates could just leave you homeless.

# Shopping Tips for Men

*December 4, 2003*

Right off the bat, this is going to sound sexist. But I want to talk to the men out there. Ladies, you can leave.

It's time for my annual shopping tips for men. I know I sound like a chauvinist, but women don't need my advice. Men do.

So guys, here it goes:

**Tip 1.** When shopping, avoid sales racks. Women huddle around sales racks. They know sales racks. You don't. They'll eat you alive. You're like a zebra wandering into a pack of Bengal tigers. Quietly back away.

**Tip 2.** If you must go to a sales rack, do not look the women in the eye. They will see your fear. And they will kill you.

**Tip 3.** Do not, I repeat, do not comparison shop. It just adds to the agony. And, like I've said, Who cares if you can find the same handbag for your wife for 20 percent less on the other side of the mall? It's on the other side of the mall. Just pay up, and get out.

**Tip 4.** Avoid stores with salespeople who want to help you look for something. If they're so damn eager, just ask 'em to do the shopping themselves. And you'll be back later.

**Tip 5.** Think perfume. For some reason, every time you buy perfume, they give you other stuff . . . little duffle bags, lipsticks. Best I can figure, this is only done with perfume purchases. I say, have at it. It looks like you went shopping for months!

**Tip 6.** Get the same exact thing for every woman on your list—mother, daughter, wife, girlfriend, aunt. Same perfume, same extra duffle bags, lipsticks.

**Tip 7.** Talk to yourself. Not only will other shoppers steer clear of you, sales people will bend over backward to rush you through your shopping and be rid of you.

**Tip 8.** Dress lightly. I've gone into malls in a winter coat, and left in nothing but my skivvies. Trust me, every mall in this country is at least 90 degrees. Think Bermuda shorts.

**Tip 9.** Cheeses and smoked meats are not bad gifts.

**Tip 10.** If Tips 1–9 overwhelm you, one word: Internet. Dress as you please.

## What Is Too Old?

*August 4, 1999*

I know we live in a youth-obsessed culture. But sometimes I kind of think we overdo it. Not that I think there's anything wrong with being young and pretty.

But what does that make the rest of us . . . old and ugly?

Maybe it's because I feel boxed in, tucked firmly by birth between the MTV generation and AARP membership.

No matter. Even I'm too old. Too old to get a leading role on a soap opera. Too old to have soda executives marketing to me. Too old to even make the cut in one of those hip potato-chip commercials.

Then I started to realize something. The problem isn't me. Maybe the problem is Madison Avenue. It's so caught up in young and sexy that it's forgotten age and character. Because if some recent surveys are right, old and wise is plenty sexy and hip.

You might have caught this survey getting a lot of press, where a bunch of folks aged forty-five and over were asked to rate their sex lives.

I won't get into the, shall I say, nitty gritty. Let me just cut to the chase . . . their sex lives are just fine, thank you. Busy. Productive. Enjoyable.

There's even this "50 Sexiest People Over 50" list that includes the likes of Robert Redford and Sophia Loren. Yet it amazes me how little attention this sort of thing gets. It's treated almost as if it's quaint.

Well, here's a news flash for ya, Madison Avenue. Character beats characters any day. I'll take tried and true over untapped and new. It's not that being young is a sin. It's more like being old, or older, is a blessing. But you wouldn't know it in our ads, or our attitudes.

Maybe because we're chasing a market we assume will spend, and ignoring the market that actually has all the dough to spend.

But this isn't just about a good market. It's about good people. Their age lines aren't scars. They are badges of honor. You don't see that in ads. You see it in their faces.

Maybe they're not the ones out of touch. Maybe, Madison Avenue, you are.

## What Is Too Vindictive?

*August 5, 1999*

Let me ask you something personal, if you don't mind. Do you hold grudges? Are you more inclined to fight than forgive?

The reason I ask is that I think Americans tend to be forgiving. Very forgiving. We're so busy turning the other cheek that sometimes it looks like our heads are spinning.

Maybe they are. And maybe that's not good. And maybe that means sometimes people can take advantage of our collective kindness.

But I digress. The reason I'm even mentioning this now is that our big old hearts are being put to one big old test. With a lot of people. And a lot of events.

Like Darryl Strawberry, who has started his comeback from cancer and a 113-day drug suspension. Never mind that New Yorkers have forgiven him for a number of missteps already. I bet they're gonna give him some slack again.

Like the restaurant Boston Chicken. Sure it's fallen on hard times, its stock reduced to pennies. But its fans are still out there. Supposedly, there's one who's ready to inject 140 million bucks into the chain.

And yes, even like Hillary Clinton. Her admittedly bizarre explanation for her husband's sexual exploits might be lost on the pundits, but it's apparently registering with everyone else as her poll numbers rise.

And who knows more about Americans' capacity to forgive than Bill Clinton himself?

My point is this: Through the worst press and the most damaging headlines, I'm always convinced that good will prevail . . . maybe too much good for what is frankly a lot of bad.

For example, the technology stocks finding no friends now will find friends again. I don't know when. And I don't know at what price.

But Americans are more apt to buy on what looks good than to punish in lemming fashion because of what looks bad.

Maybe that's what led us to victory in World War II—realizing, against all odds, that you can either curse the darkness or look forward to the light.

Like I've said, I'd much rather be naïve and upbeat than smart and dour.

## Why I'd Buy a Casket . . . at Costco

*August 17, 2004*

So Costco is selling caskets. I thought I had died and gone to heaven.

Sorry, I couldn't help myself.

But lest you think this is a tacky thing, I think it's a good thing. I know the funeral home industry thinks it's awful. One operator says it will only mean he'll have to hike his costs. I have no idea why. I mean, you can shop for cars and computers and compare. Why not caskets?

And you might really love Aunt Sophie, but who says she has to leave this world in a five-thousand-dollar box when you can get the same box for thousands less?

I don't mean to be crass, but if we're dying to save money when we're alive, we should be dying to save it when we're, well, dead.

I have nothing against funeral homes. But let's face it, they're doing business with people at their most vulnerable moment. I've been there myself. And you're generally in no mood to comparison shop. Often, you just want to get through it. And I suspect funeral operators know it.

So here's what I say: While you're alive, plan on being dead.

I knew a business guy who made all the arrangements for his goodbye years before he actually said his goodbyes. He arranged everything from the casket, the mass cards, right down to the people he wanted to speak at his funeral! He even prearranged no flowers!

We have a lot of hang-ups about death in this country. That's partly why it's become such a big business for us. Oftentimes people shell out as much for a funeral as they do for a car. The difference is that the car goes places. That casket goes only one place.

I say, competition's good. You may love Aunt Sophie a lot. But that doesn't mean her funeral should cost a lot. Now don't get me wrong, this doesn't mean that you should throw Aunt Sophie in a cardboard box and make the funeral a drive-through. It does mean that you should start preparing ahead of time. And if I know Aunt Sophie, prudent in her life, I'll bet she'd appreciate you being prudent . . . in her death.

Me? I want to be buried in a big Wendy's wrapper. And just this last time? Hold the sides!

## Conned for Cash?

*June 17, 1999*

Tell me if this has ever happened to you. You get a big sweepstakes announcement telling you you've won. Ten million smackers are comin' your way! And all of a sudden you're feeling woozy. You're practicing your take-this-job-and-shove-it speech for the boss.

And while you're dancing through the kitchen, something catches the corner of your twinkling eye . . . a wee, tiny line just below that bellowing picture of Ed McMahon that says, ". . . if you are among the finalists chosen."

Suddenly your dreary middle-class life is put back into alarming focus.

Damn!

Apparently this skit has been played out in thousands— make that millions—of American households. And if some attorney generals have things their way, it's gonna stop.

A bunch of 'em want to start what you might call "sweepstakes standards." Right up front you'll be told about the odds of winning that big prize—more often than not, as high as nearly 200 million to one! You'll also be told that you don't have to purchase something to win something, or even improve your odds of winning something.

What's got these AGs screaming "Louise" is this: A lot of Louises and Lous are being played for suckers. Particularly elderly Louises and Lous, many of whom believe what they read and assume a big prize is theirs.

And who can blame them? Sometimes the fine print is so fine that I don't think Ken Starr could find it. So don't blame the elderly for being gullible. Blame these contest organizers for being galling.

Maybe a lot of folks are trusting, and maybe some are too trusting. But that doesn't give you license to take advantage of 'em. So put it in writing. Big writing. And make it clear. Just because Ed says so . . . doesn't make it so.


## Have Beeper, Will Travel

*May 24, 1999*

Let me be very clear about this. No one, anywhere, will ever be able to go on vacation the same way again.

You heard me right. The days of ditching the office for a little R & R are now over. Not when companies like 3Com tout wireless e-mailing with gadgets like the new Palm 7. Or when Motorola sports a phone that can be used anywhere on earth, from even the most remote jungle. And not when titans like Microsoft promise a means of getting that data anywhere on God's green earth.

You get the point. You can reach your office anytime. More important, they can reach you anytime. When you're sunning on the beach, wading in that pond in New Hampshire, kayaking through the Grand Canyon.

They can get you. Reach you. Nag you. Anytime. Anywhere.

It's that easy. That annoying. And that permanent.

In a way, we're all like the president of the United States now. Remember those pictures of Ronald Reagan chopping wood or clearing brush on his California ranch, years back? I used to watch that and figure, "Gosh, he can't get out of the spotlight's way." Or the pictures of President Clinton caught munching a double ice cream cone, spilling some on his shirt for the world to see?

I don't know if everyone will watch our every move. But this much I do know: They'll be able to, because it's a lot easier to.

Not good if you're trying to get away from it all. Very good if your biggest worry was leaving the office in the first place.

## Lessons from Maria

*April 14, 1999*

Maria Grasso never had it easy. A fifty-four-year-old Chilean immigrant, she was doing all she could do just to make ends meet. Kind of tough when you're a single mom with two kids in college. Tougher still when the jobs you want aren't the jobs you get. And then the jobs you do get aren't the jobs that pay a lot. But you do what you can, however you can do it.

Maria tried it all. She was a teaching assistant, working with mentally handicapped kids. Then she was a nanny of sorts for the children of a multimillionaire. It wasn't so bad, she said. She always loved kids, and someday, she figured, she'd like to help them more.

Now, Maria Grasso can. In case you didn't hear, this live-in babysitter has just come forward to claim the largest lottery prize ever won by an individual: $197 million. Maria's taking the dough in one lump sum. That works out to $70 million, after taxes.

True to form, Maria doesn't know what she's going to do with this newfound manna from heaven. But she has an idea. "I'd like to help kids," she told reporters. "Especially troubled kids—kids who really need the help."

Seventy million dollars can help you do a lot. But the fact that Maria isn't talking about doing a lot for herself probably says a lot about her . . . and maybe offers hope for the rest of us.

Money's nice, let's face it. But doing nice things with it . . . well, that's even nicer.

## A Roll of Dough or a Roll in the Hay?

*December 14, 1998*

If I offered you the choice of a million dollars or a better sex life, what would you choose? Well, if you're among those surveyed in January's *Redbook* magazine, you'd opt for the dough.

Seventy-eight percent of husbands and 84 percent of wives chose money under the mattress over doing anything on the mattress.

The fact that more women than men wanted the mil' is another issue. For now, let me focus on the bigger one. Money matters. I'm not here to explain why . . . Just to say, as a business guy at Fox, that I'm not surprised.

Maybe those who voted for the mil' figure that money's the greatest aphrodisiac anyway. Clearly, cash is a turn-on. I'm reminded of that old Bea Arthur line—that, given the choice of marrying poor but happy versus rich but sad, she'd still opt for the latter.

Money can't buy you happiness. And this time of year, it can't guarantee a great holiday. But it's so desirable . . . which means, I guess, that I'm desirable. After all, up until this *Redbook* survey, I was just a business nerd. I'm still a nerd. But I take some solace in imagining myself a sexy one. Something to sleep on . . . only to sleep on.

## How to Know If Your Boss Is a Jerk

*July 8, 2002*

You know, we got so much reaction to my "Five Great Things to Look for in a Boss" that I'm now offering this sequel, "Five Dead Giveaway Signs That Your Boss Is a Crook":

**Sign #1.** He or she doesn't look you straight in the eye. Something's wrong there. Why? When I was a kid and did something wrong, I tended to look down a lot just before my dad launched me into orbit. It was bad in a kid. It's worse in a boss.

**Sign #2.** The boss is spending less time at work. I'm not talking traveling on business. He's just not there, period. Why? Is he preparing an exit, or is something more sinister afoot?

**Sign #3.** When the big cheese is at work, he or she spends a lot of time with creepy people. People who don't talk much, and certainly don't talk to you. People who make it clear that they know, and you don't. And now they're powwowing with the boss. Be afraid. Be very afraid.

**Sign #4.** He or she starts avoiding any and all media interviews. If it ain't an earnings-quiet period, why so darn quiet? What's he cooking up? Speaking of cooking up . . .

**Sign #5.** Your boss doesn't show up at the annual picnic . . . if he even bothers with such things in the first place. That should tell you one of two things. Either he can't be bothered with you, or the burgers you're eating are poisoned.

Any one of these signs makes the boss suspect. Two or more, a little dicey. Three . . . lock him up. All five? Throw away the freakin' key!

# CHAPTER 15

# *RIGHT TO LIFE*

*I* don't hide it. No doubt I've lost viewers—and maybe some readers of this very book—because of it. But I come down on the side of life. Every time. Every issue. Every day. Maybe it's my Catholic upbringing, but I've framed our existence on this earth as a shared and blessed gift from way beyond this earth. It's a gift we all must treasure, and it's a gift we all must protect.

Some see it as interfering. I see it as respecting . . . all life, all the time. I think a society degrades itself when it starts trying to parse out the question of exactly what life is, or what exactly an acceptable life is. It's a slippery slope, and a dangerous one.

The greatest societies are invariably the most caring ones— the ones that look after their elderly, yet honor their young. Some say I'm black-and-white on this matter. They're right. I am. And on issues that go way beyond the economics of the matter, I try to get to the heart of the matter.

## Why Terri Schiavo Matters

*March 22, 2005*

Look, things like life and death are deeply personal decisions. And I think both sides of this Terri Schiavo case are arguing deeply held and honestly held convictions.

So I'm not here to yell. Or shout. Or be a demagogue.

No one knows what Terri's thinking. Even if she's thinking. We do know, for now, that she is alive. Maybe years and years ago, she would have wished herself dead if she could see herself alive like she is today. We just don't know for sure. Her husband says one thing, her parents another.

And a nation rushes to make out living wills so that their intentions are never in doubt.

My only question is: what, ultimately, is life?

If you were to tell a twenty-something that when she was a forty-something she'd have a debilitating disease that would slowly sap her strength, her ability to walk and see, and even think and move; that this disease would only worsen and likely kill her, she might ask to put in writing: Kill me first.

But many who deal with such debilitating issues fight on. Live on. Carry on. And go on. Just like the soldier who could never envision a life without arms or legs, who somehow adjusts and rues the day he ever thought of ending that life.

Life means different things to different people. I don't think it's a bad thing to cling to. Even if the life we cling to isn't perfect.

For me, this much is clear: I think our presumed bias should be toward life. Let other countries explore euthanasia and killing someone mercifully. My fear is that the acts will become less merciful. Something is very wrong in a country that throws you in jail for neglecting to give your dog food and water, but couldn't care less if you do the same . . . to a human being.

## For the Life of Me . . . What About Life?

*July 19, 2004*

Did you ever read or catch something in the news that was so stupid, so asinine, that right then and there you threw up your hands or just screamed, or just threw up your hands and screamed?

It happened to me last week, reading a column in the *New York Times Magazine*. It was about this woman Amy Richards (as told to Amy Barrett), who was pregnant with triplets. You'd think that was wonderful news. But not to Amy. She wanted to know if there was a way she could have just one of the babies. She shares her conversation with her doctor: "Is it possible to get rid of one of them? Or two of them?"

She coolly, almost icily, explains how her obstetrician—although she wasn't an expert in "selective reduction"—knew that "with a shot of potassium chloride you could eliminate one or more." I couldn't believe what I was reading. This woman was seriously considering aborting two perfectly fine fetuses, whether her boyfriend liked it or not. And here's the kicker: The boyfriend didn't like it. He had heard the three heartbeats on the sonogram. He wanted the triplets. To which she snipped: "This is why they say it's the woman's choice, because you think I could just carry triplets."

Apparently Amy tells her boyfriend it isn't easy being pregnant, let alone carrying triplets. Fine for him to tell her to have 'em, I guess, but he's not the one who would likely have to be put on bed rest at twenty weeks, or be forced to shop at Costco to buy big jars of mayonnaise. (Heaven forbid!)

No, this poor schmuck who got her knocked up in the first place can't possibly relate to how Amy's poor life will be turned upside down. He can't fathom the inconvenience or societal pressures. He has no voice in this matter. And she is happy with that.

I'm incredulous as I go on reading, learning of the procedure that wipes out two innocent lives. She ends up having a boy and reports, "Everything is fine." Maybe for that little boy, I think to myself. But not for the others. They never had a chance. What amazes me is that this woman was perfectly willing to go through nine months of a pregnancy and deliver a human being into this world. And that what she wouldn't do was put up with the discomfort—social and otherwise—of bringing two others along for the ride. They're gone. They're history. They're . . . dead.

I don't believe I've ever read anything so chilling and dismissive. And yet it's freely placed in a prominent column in one of the world's most prominent newspapers. It troubles me deeply, and worries me even more deeply. It's not just the callous indifference to life, but the very idea of something we might call "convenient life." It wasn't convenient for this woman to have those two other kids. So obliterate them. Remove them. Kill them.

I'm thinking about all the couples out there, desperate for kids—any kid in any state of health—who would gladly walk into that delivery room and take those two burdens off Amy's shoulders. But no, Amy didn't give those prospective parents a chance, just like she never gave those two babies a chance.

I'm biased. I'm dead set against abortion. But even I try to understand extenuating circumstances. If Amy had said, "I don't want to be pregnant, no how, no way," I could see it. I would better understand her decision to abort the whole damn litter. But no, she aborted two beings, and kept one, almost as if she were sifting through ears of corn at the grocery store, throwing in her cart the ears she wanted, passing over the ears she did not.

The difference there, of course, is that other shoppers can choose from those other ears. But Amy didn't give those other shoppers the choice or the chance. She scorched the earth. She scorched the possibilities. She scorched . . . us.

Amy Richards tells Amy Barrett of not knowing what she'll do if she ever becomes pregnant again: "I would do the same thing if I had triplets again, but if I had twins, I would probably have twins." Thanks, Amy, it's nice to know how your mind works. And it's nice to know how the *New York Times* works, giving prominence to this woman's odd cherry-picking of life.

I know that in this day and age abortion is the law of the land. Some swear by it. Others at it. I'm just shocked when I see in black and white how some parse it, and select it, even extol it. As if it were a good thing. Is it me, or am I the only one in the country who can only fathom this as a sick thing, a very sick thing?

Then again, I'm just a man. And as Amy seemed to surmise to the other Amy, this is just a life. The life you choose. And the two . . . you do not.

# Not Sheepish About Life

### February 24, 1997

I'll say this about Wall Street traders: They are not a sheepish lot. And I mean that literally. With all the hullabaloo over researchers in Scotland cloning a grown sheep, buyers are cloning themselves in droves and surgically attaching themselves to any company having anything to do with this.

Take PPL Therapeutics, the teeny-tiny biotechnology company that helped fund Dr. Ian Wilmut, the scientist who led the cloning team. PPL shares surged more than 15 percent today, largely on optimism that these guys aren't just cloning around.

Nor are American Home Products or Denmark's Novo Nordisk. Both have research deals with PPL on other non-cloning matters. But what the hey—if the connection fits, clone it, or buy it, or whatever.

It's a remarkable turn of events—and one that all but ignores the ethical rage that this little sheep has sparked.

Is it right to clone and play God? Is it right to clone animals and play doctor? Who knows? That's the stuff of philosophical and theological debate—concepts as alien to Wall Street as a bear . . . in sheep's clothing.

## CHAPTER 16

# *RANTS!*

*M*y Irish mom, knowing full well that her Italian-Irish son had a temper, would tell me that you can tell the measure of a man by what bugs him. Little slights, little man, she would say. She never said whether or not a guy who agitates at bigger slights was, by definition, a bigger man.

I try to save my own temper and passions for the things that are bigger or, at least, big to me. Some call them pet peeves. Others might say pet rants. For me, I guess you'd call them pet causes. They might be stories in the news, or developments that may someday be news. But if it's on my mind, before viewers know it, it's likely to be on my show.

## Lawyers

*May 22, 2000*

Thieving SOBs.

I'm sorry, I don't know any other way to say it.

I am angry. Very angry. Flyin' off the handle and throwing anything in sight angry. And who am I angry at?

Lawyers.

Not all lawyers. Just the ones who in good conscience are collecting billions of dollars in fees for their work in that $246-billion national tobacco deal, which worked out to some doozie of a deal for them.

According to court records, which are only now becoming available, a lot of these guys are cleaning up. As *USA Today* reports, their fees work out to something close to seven thousand dollars per hour. And that's in Louisiana alone. More than ten billion smackers nationally.

Now don't get me wrong. A lot of these private law firms who banded together to take on the big, bad tobacco titans deserve something for their efforts.

But ten billion bucks! I don't think so, Sparky. Because you don't have to be Perry Mason to know tobacco's buckling.

But you do have to be something close to the Antichrist to take money out of the hands of kids—especially when kids were the ones who were supposed to benefit from all this tobacco dough.

I mean, ask yourself this: What about all those programs that were supposed to stop our sons and daughters from smoking? By my math, they'll be getting money. But for the moment their lawyers are getting money first. And that's what is so sickening about this.

Don't get me wrong. I like lawyers. Some of my best friends are lawyers. But I don't like greedy thieves. And some of these guys are greedy thieves. Anyone ever hear of a sliding scale for these types of mammoth rewards? Well, the lawyers involved seem to have a two-word response: "Slide this."

And these guys have the nerve to say the tobacco industry is trying to fill its coffers on the backs of unsuspecting customers.

Well, call me clueless, but I don't know who's worse—the devil you know, or the lawyer who painted him that way. Either one makes my skin crawl.

## Stick to Acting

*July 21, 2004*

I'm not usually one to offer Hollywood stars tips. So, consider this a freebie.

If your career's floundering, bash Bush. You heard me right. You want your name in the paper? Knock the guy in the White House. Works like a charm. Every time.

Don't believe me?

Look at Linda Ronstadt. I had no idea she was even still singing until I heard about her Bush-ranting.

Now she's in the news. And getting something every celebrity craves . . . attention. Who cares if she was thrown out of the Aladdin in Vegas. She's been thrown into the national debate. And I betcha she's loving every minute of it.

Then there's Whoopi Goldberg. Her show's not a hit. So she hits the president. Becomes a hit in the press. Unfortunately, gets hit at Slim Fast. No matter, Whoopie's a hit with the left. She needn't worry about her career. They'll take good care of her.

After all, nothing juices up a career like a little controversy. It worked for the Dixie Chicks when they went after the president. Dumb move there, of course, since their core audience seems to like the president. No matter, the Chicks clicked in the press. For a little while, at least.

Just be careful. Not all attention is good attention.

Just look at Sinead O'Connor. She rips up a picture of the Pope, and before you know it, Ireland's answer to Curly from the Three Stooges now can't see a news hit for a song hit.

But them there's the breaks. You belt out something other than a song, don't be surprised if your fans belt out something other than applause. Celebrities are free, of course, to rant all they want, because they say they care. Just as their fans are free to say, "Shut the hell up." Because we don't.

# Hey, Theater Owners! Can the Commercials!

*July 2, 2004*

Have any of you been to a movie theater lately?

It's ridiculous. It's out of control. I'm not talking about Michael Moore's film. I'm not even talking about films, period. I'm talking about the commercials! They're everywhere.

And they're over the top. Too long. Too many. Too much.

Movie theaters say they need 'em to defray the cost of tickets for the viewing public. That's a lie. A bold-faced lie. I don't know about you, but my ticket prices aren't getting any cheaper!

That lie is about as bad as the one that says a show is going to start at 8 P.M. No, what these sniveling, phony, ticket-pushing pimps don't tell you is that it's the commercials that start at 8 P.M. Once you get past them and the previews, you're looking at 8:15 P.M.—at the earliest!

Look, I have no problem with advertising in places and on shows where I expect it. But not in theaters, where I do not. And, I think, where I should not.

Look, I know theater owners gotta make money. But guys, you gotta try something more novel: the truth!

I'll tell ya what. If you argue that these commercials are defraying your costs, give us a choice. Pay more for a movie without the commercials. Or less for a movie with 'em.

I dare you.

I dare you to be honest and not the sneaky worms so many of you theater chains have become. Maybe some moviegoers will happily endure the ads for a better price on a flick. Or maybe some will just tell you to flick off. Their choice. Not yours.

# Hey Doc! See Me!

*December 16, 2003*

Tell me if this has ever happened to you: You walk into a doctor's office. Let them know you're there for a 10:30 appointment. The receptionist, without looking up, reminds you to sign the register and be seated. You sign the register. You take your seat. And you wait.

And you wait some more. And you keep waiting some more.

The waiting room is crowded. There's not a spare seat to be had. It's Grand Central Station at rush hour. And everyone's coughing.

The guy next to you seems to have expired.

Some thirty minutes into this ordeal, you ask the other fellow next to you, just out of curiosity, how long he's been waiting.

"About an hour," he says.

"What time was your appointment?" you ask.

"Ten thirty" he confirms.

"Mine too," the guy next to him chimes in.

"Me too," blurts out the guy next to you—the one you thought was dead. Just sleeping, it turns out.

Suddenly it dawns on you. Everyone in that waiting room has the same exact appointment. Yet they dutifully wait.

I can only assume because this must be the only doctor on the planet.

But I realize something. This is not the only doctor on the planet. And he is being rude.

Other doctors tell me doctors get busy. Doctors get surprise patients. Sick patients. I lose patience with this patient argument.

I ask the receptionist what the problem is.

She shrugs. "He's busy, I guess."

"And we're not?" I ask.

Would it kill that doctor to give us some information? Just a simple instruction to his receptionist: "Please tell those out there that I'm running late . . . and apologize for me."

None of that. No time for that. But plenty of time to keep patients stewing and sick people wondering, Will I die waiting to see my doctor?

I wish I could tell you how it worked out. But I left. I don't know what the other patients did. I fear the least the guy next to me never got out of there alive.

I'll tell you this. I have a show at 4 P.M. Eastern. Silly me, I show up at 4 P.M. Eastern! So Doc, I know you're saving lives, but save us the song and dance. You might make a lot of dollars and cents. But for my money, you haven't a damn bit of common sense. So many fancy-schmancy degrees, and not a one . . . in humility.

## When Hands-On Guys Go Hands-Off

*January 27, 2005*

So now Bernie Ebbers says he never was a numbers guy. As his WorldCom fraud trial begins, his defense seems to be, "I was in charge, but I wasn't in charge."

Funny—when companies are soaring and the money and praise are rolling in, the guy on top is in charge and hands-on. Suddenly, when the you-know-what hits the fan, he's out of the loop and hands-off.

Ken Lay appears to be taking much the same defense at Enron. Ditto Dennis Kozlowski at Tyco.

When all those companies were hummin', I didn't hear one of them bummin'. Stymied about numbers they didn't know. They knew 'em all. About businesses they didn't comprehend. They comprehended 'em all.

I guess it's human nature. When things are good, we like to take all the credit. When they're going bad, we like someone else to take all the blame. But it seems pretty transparent to me.

I'm impressed by the CEOs who brag about their great teams and people when things are going well—but who fault their own miscues when they do not.

When Jack Welch failed to merge with Honeywell, he said, in effect, "I botched it." I was impressed.

Just like I was when Lee Iacocca came on board at Chrysler and admitted that quality was a problem with some of his cars, but not any of his people. He leaned on them to produce better cars, and they did. And when the company produced better numbers, he sang their praises.

Good bosses know bad things can happen. Great bosses are big enough to admit them and take responsibility for them . . . when they do.

## CHAPTER 17

# *BEING UPBEAT!*

*I* know it sounds trite, even clichéd, but I'm a big believer in being upbeat. I once approached life from the opposite direction, and it was simply too depressing.

When I was first diagnosed with multiple sclerosis in the fall of 1997, I was bitter and angry at the world. It wasn't just because I had only recently beaten back cancer, but because I had already seen so much illness and death in my family. No one escaped my temper or my nonstop carping nature.

My wife finally had to tell me I was hell to be around. Eventually I straightened up and started looking up. I have never looked back. None of this newfound positivism has made my MS go away. It's still here, every day. I'm just better able to cope every day, because I whine less, and focus on the good more.

That doesn't mean I still don't vent. I just make it a point to vent soon, vent fast, and vent often. I try to be honest. I try to be direct. But throughout, I try to put it all in perspective, taking nothing personally, seeing no one as contemptible (save maybe the French), and seeing life itself as enjoyable. Here's the bad side of it: it can't stop me from lecturing, even if it's all in good-natured fun.

## The Bad Boss, the Good Response

*March 23, 2004*

Many years ago I worked for a guy who was miserable. I mean, *miserable*. He was demeaning and dictatorial. He loved to make himself look good, and anyone who worked for him look small.

He was curt, rude, condescending, and nasty. I always felt he got off by acting like he had your number. He didn't have mine. I vowed never to let him ruin my day, or my work.

He seemed to sense my indifference to his indifference, and one day he called me into his office.

"You don't like me, do you?" he asked.

"No, I don't," he said.

"Why?" he asked.

"Because I don't like the way you make other people feel," I said.

He never fired me or even berated me. To this day, I don't know what he made of me. He moved on. I moved on.

But I learned something then about how to deal with the kind of people who would love to bring us down now. Far be it from me to compare this old boss to terrorist groups, but there is a connection. So bear with me.

Terrorist groups love to intimidate us. They want to make us nervous. They want us down. They want us worried. They want us sick. They want our number.

I say, don't give it to them. Some people love nothing more than having you wallow in the misery that is their lives. We should do better with our lives.

It's easy to live our lives in fear. It's better to live our lives in hope. Bad bosses don't get that. Terrorists never want us to see that. Each, I suspect, would kill to force that.

It is up to us to prove that we are bigger than that. We can look at life and say it fills just half a glass. Or we can look at them, and rightly conclude, they're just half-assed.

## Aunt Molly's St. Patty's Day Message

*March 17, 2004*

On Saint Patrick's Day, I always remember my Aunt Molly. She was right off the sod, as Irish as Irish could be. I can remember her thick Irish brogue as if she were still alive today.

"Neil," she would say. "You've got a grand noggin . . . just try not to act like it."

Even back then, my family ribbed me about my head!

She played a very large role in my life, very close to my Irish mom, very close to my family. She was always calling, always writing.

I don't think a week went by in college or grad school that I didn't get a letter or package from Aunt Molly. On St. Patty's Day, she'd always send me Irish soda bread. I hated soda bread, and always tried to pass it off to my Italian dad, who really hated Irish soda bread.

But I digress. She'd warn me about the evils of college and "loose women." Can you imagine what she'd think of me interviewing Playboy bunnies?

But what I remember is her advice on life.

"A great man," she would tell me, "doesn't need to act great. He thanks the Lord for his gifts . . . and stays humble."

But her best line was one she repeated quite often, and she repeated it once more to me right before her death.

"Neil, laugh at yourself . . . because you know everyone else is."
She'd smile. And I'd smile. She got it. I get it.
Happy St. Patty's Day.

# Why I'm a Pollyanna, and Proud of It!

*March 5, 2004*

You know I get a lot of critical e-mail here. Often, it's for being too optimistic . . . too "rose-colored-glassish," as one viewer put it.

You know what? You're right.

I do have a very different take on things. It's much more up-beat than others you're hearing in the media.

Take a look at the economic numbers. Why do we focus on the downside all the time? The media sees a 5.6 percent unemployment rate and calls it bad. I see a 94.4 percent employment rate and I call it pretty good.

The media says only 21,000 jobs were added to the economy. I see six months straight of job gains in this economy. And more than 360,000 jobs at that. Happens all the time.

I hear a lot about a few corporate crooks. But I hear nothing about the thousands of publicly listed companies that aren't crooks.

I hear a good deal about the one-and-a-half percent of bad priests, but never, not once, anything remotely positive about the 98-and-a-half percent who are good priests.

I hear that every mutual fund is rigged, yet I discover more than nine out of ten are not. I know we like to report on the one plane in ten million that crashes. Or the car accident that stops traffic.

Perhaps reports of the positive things aren't as compelling. Imagine the headlines: "Yet Another Plane Landed Safely Today," or "99.9 Percent of People Made it Home Today."

If it bleeds, it leads. If it corrupts, it counts. If it distorts, it dominates.

I don't know.

This much I do know. That the world I see isn't nearly as bad as the *reports* I see. Things are not perfect, but they are far from pathetic. If that makes me a Pollyanna, then color me rosy. But get a lot of paint. After all, this is a pretty big head.

## Why I Like Steve Ballmer

*August 16, 2001*

I like leaders who are unconventional. Leaders who are passionate. Who laugh. Who yell. Who enjoy life. And make you enjoy life too.

Steve Ballmer's a cheerleader, and a darn good one. And I think that's what a leader should be. The best ones are.

Jack Welch of General Electric had that special magic, that enthusiasm and aura that transcended the stiff CEO. He inspired. He laughed. At you. At himself. But he really loved what he did. And it showed.

You don't have to agree with everything a CEO does or says. But the first question for me is, does this guy make me want to go to work at his company?

Nothing seems mundane to them. Or boring to them. Or tedious to them. Or a waste of time to them.

It's like that old Ted Baxter line, when he was trying to console Mary Richards when she was going through a funk.

"Mary," he suggested. "I just don't get up in the morning and brush my teeth and wash my face and put my clothes on . . . I *get up in the morning* and *brush my teeth* and *wash my face* and *put my clothes on!*"

Even old Ted Baxter got it right. It's not the drudgery of the day-to-day we should consider, but how lucky we are that we have it in the first place.

# When Little Guys Strike It Big

*March 17, 1999*

I must admit, I'm an incredible romantic, and perhaps a bit too much of an idealist. Gosh, my eyes well up at Kodak commercials.

My point is that I'm a sucker for a poignant story. So imagine what someone like me would make of this Goldman Sachs share-the-wealth story.

In case you didn't hear, the last big private partnership on Wall Street is going public. And it's only now revealing how it will divide its $24 billion in projected net worth.

Now I already knew that General Partners, who own the firm, stand to make at least $50 million smackers each. What I didn't know is that they're not the only ones benefiting. Secretaries are too. And janitors. And lowly office assistants. And researchers. And copiers. Even the kids who make the late-night pizza runs. They're *all* sharing in this newfound wealth.

Most will receive at least half their annual salary in some lump-sum bonus. That ain't chicken feed. And for a lot of these hard-working men and women, it's all the money in the world.

No, it ain't $50 million. And for some, maybe not more than ten thousand bucks. And for others, likely a little more. But it's something. Maybe it's tuba lessons for the secretary's kid. Or a dream vacation for the hard-working word processor. Or maybe just a little security for a janitor and his family.

Now if that ain't a Kodak moment, I don't know what is. Pass the tissues.

## A Different Kind of Midlife Crisis

*February 17, 1999*

Sometimes it's nice to knock conventional wisdom on its head. Take this long-held view of the forty-something male going through a midlife crisis. You know the score. Frantic with his lot in life, he turns that life upside down.

He ditches the loyal wife, buys himself a sports car, and scoops up a trophy girlfriend. Usually blonde, usually bubbly.

Turns out that while a few guys might do that, the vast majority do not. And not just guys. Women too, are not nearly so shallow or so self-absorbed as to go just crazy because they're getting just old.

You've no doubt heard about this study that shows the vast majority of these forty-to-sixty somethings truly are something.

Oh yes, they like the good life. But they want to share it with someone, usually the same someone who was with them when they didn't have a good life.

And they like toys, but not nearly as much as their kids and grandkids.

And get this, they actually like getting old. Sure they miss that twenty-something body, but not at the expense of that well-seasoned fifty- or sixty-something mind.

Theirs has been a bumpy journey, but to hear the vast majority tell it, a fun one. And a fun one to come.

Stereotypes are tough to shatter. And no doubt, we'll still demonize those skirt-chasing, Corvette-driving, midlife thundering execs in daytime dramas.

Just so long as we know those are daytime dramas . . . and not reality.


## Why Sad Faces Equal Slow Economy

*November 11, 1998*

Are moods contagious? The reason I ask is that there's a study out that says spouses end up "mimicking" the mood of their partners.

If one's upset, the other gets upset. If one's elated, the other gets elated. Not all the time, but enough, apparently, to convince doctors that our mothers were right—you are the company you keep.

Which gets me back to Wall Street. I don't know if you've been following things lately, but a lot of brokerage firms are laying off a lot of people. More than three thousand at Merrill Lynch. Fifteen hundred at Bankers Trust. Eight thousand at Citigroup!

Now you don't have to be Sigmund Freud to find that depressing. Not only for the people losing their jobs, but even for the ones sticking around. They might wonder, "Am I next?"

Suddenly it clouds their world, blurs their vision. So isn't it odd that when I look at a lot of these brokerage house reports on the economy, they talk of severe slowdown, of the drastic need for the Fed to cut rates, and of the dire state of the world today.

Maybe a lot of it's true. And maybe a lot of the world is ill. But when your own glass looks half-empty, it's very hard to see things half-full.

And it's the half-empty glass the crowd is presenting us now. The same crowd that's down and just might want us to feel the same way. Now, ain't that a pain in the glass!

## Forget the Gipper, Just Go for a Smiler

*November 17, 1998*

You know, they have actually done studies that prove what we already know: We like people who smile. People who smile are fun to be around. Which I guess means that people who don't smile aren't fun to be around.

Which gets me back to Republicans. They way I figure it, they desperately need a smiler. Someone who can make us laugh. Or at least make us feel good.

Ronald Reagan had that unique skill. As Lee Walczak points out in the latest *Business Week,* the old Gipper had a way of giving conservatism a smiling face. Walczak goes on to point out that this year's role models are the beaming Bush boys, Texas governor George W. and Florida's Jeb.

We tend to tolerate even bitter medicine when it's administered by a friendly doctor. Indeed, we'll forgive a lot if the messenger means well. Remember how the Bay of Pigs fiasco didn't even touch the resolutely funny, resolutely popular John Kennedy.

So there you have it—my cheap advice for the Grand Old Party. Put on a grand old happy face. And watch what happens.

## CHAPTER 18

# *BEING RIGHT*

*E*arly on, I promised that I would show myself, warts and all, in this book—the good calls I've made, and the bad calls I've made. I just chose to hold off on the details until we got this deep in the book, so that you could digest the message of my heart before I asked you to deal with the more inconsistent messages of my mind.

Looking back on it, I'm somewhat amazed by the things I did see coming—including a huge bubble building in stocks in the late 1990s—as well as the things I didn't see coming . . . like the exact names of those bubble stocks that were building in the 1990s. Some of my core positions were built on simple, but inarguable truths I discovered in my years covering Wall Street. Others were gleaned simply by reading and researching the everyday life I'll simply call Main Street.

The calls are my own. The insights are my own. The things I got right are the things I like to call . . . my favorite chapter.

## Wrestling with the Truth

### May 21, 1999

No, I don't know if this is a sign of a market top. But Vince McMahon is going public.

Vince, you'll recall, is the oh-so-savvy marketing guy behind the World Wrestling Federation. And now, reports have it that Vince—the man who impeccably timed both the theater and the hype of wrestling into a cottage industry—is parlaying all that into serious talks with Bear Stearns to launch an I-P-O—sort of like an initial pounding offering.

According to *Variety*, investors would get a stab at 20 percent of Vince's empire, which could be worth hundreds of millions. But before any of you laugh, take note: Vince makes money. Lots of money. No earnings-deprived Internet startup here. Helped by sexy centerfold stars like Sable and WWF champ Stone Cold Steve Austin, Vince need not wince. His WWF just cleared 230 million smackers, and, according to *Variety*, had $50 million in cash flow.

His syndicated matches are seen around the world in some 120 countries, with 100 million viewers. And what do you think those shows and home videos make? Try 350 million bucks.

And as a separate piece in the *New York Post* points out, that doesn't even include pay-per-view or licensing. Not bad for a guy who turned a rough-and-tumble sport into a Greek tragedy on steroids—loud, raucous, funny, macabre, and big. Very big.

So when others say we've truly lost our senses if old Vince goes public, consider this: Vince makes money, a lot of Internet guys don't. Vince has Sable, a lot of Internet guys lust for Sable. And unlike nerdy, pencil-protecting web guys, Vince's guys are huge. And strong. And soon, rich. Very rich.

Is this a bull market, or what?!

# 10K Not OK

*March 18, 1999*

I don't want to rain on this Dow 10,000 parade, but I think I know what's going to undo it and the entire bull market: trade.

You heard me. Trade. Or lack of trade, I should say. The problem isn't us buying stuff from guys abroad. It's those guys abroad buying stuff from us. Right now, they aren't—at least, not nearly as much as we're buying from them.

I don't know if you caught this, but the U.S. trade deficit—the gap between what we buy from those guys and what they buy from us—ballooned in January to nearly 17 billion smackers. That's a record!

The problem isn't us. No, the problem's those guys. They just don't buy, period.

And the way we see it, their governments aren't helping matters. We say countries like France, Germany, Brazil, and Russia bend over backwards to keep things like U.S. steel and bananas out, and their steel and bananas in.

Sufficiently ticked off, we threaten sanctions and tariffs. They don't accept our bananas, we won't accept their sweaters and handbags. They don't want our steel, we set limits on steel from them.

The trouble with trade tiffs is that they invariably get nastier. Before you know it, prices start skyrocketing. Buyers stop buying. Companies stop profiting. And markets . . . well, markets just stop.

Logic tells you that cooler heads will prevail. But cooler heads haven't. And neither has logic . . . Dow 10,000 or not.

# When the Most Money Doesn't Mean the Most Brains

*January 22, 1999*

Let me tell you about Scott, a buddy of mine in college. Probably one of the most ethical guys I ever knew.

I remember one time a professor offering us a chance to take a test open-book. I hate to admit it, but I jumped at the chance. Not Scott, though. He insisted he'd do it the hard way. Turns out, when we got the tests back, Scott got a B, and I got an A. In fact, that semester I got a better grade in that class than Scott did, all because I took the test open-book, and Scott didn't.

Now who was really the smarter guy? Hey, I'm not ashamed to admit it: Scott was, hands-down. But sometimes honor doesn't win the race. Which gets me back to the Internet.

You can knock these stocks all you want. Knock the fact that their stock prices are out of sync with their profits, or lack of profits. No matter, those who have these easy moneymakers in their portfolios are kickin' butt, and those who don't are just kickin' themselves.

So now, even guys who swore they would never, ever, ever touch these earnings-challenged stocks are buying 'em. Turns out everyone from Fidelity Magellan to Transamerica Premier and Janus Mercury and Olympus funds are scooping up names like At-Home and Excite and America Online with the same glee I felt going into that open book test. I guess they figure, better a fast and easy A than an honorable B, or worse.

# Kick the Can

*January 8, 1999*

Do any of you remember that old *Twilight Zone* episode called "Kick the Can"? It was about all these residents in an old folks' rest home who went out in the middle of the night to play a game of kick the can. All except one.

Suddenly they all become kids again. All except the one sullen, serious, curmudgeon who said it was a waste of time . . . until he saw that the others had turned into children.

I thought of that show recently when I was looking at these Internet stocks. In one day, 50-60-80-point jumps for issues like Broadcast.com or Amazon.com. These Web issues are up, just this week, to an average of 30 percent. Thirty percent in one week!

And I began to wonder what established CEOs like Jack Welch or Sandy Weill think of all this. Neither is exactly a slouch, or a failure. Each has richly rewarded his shareholders. But nothing like the 1,000 percent or more returns for those sticking with these new wunderkind stocks for little more than a year or two.

Jack and Sandy wear ties. A lot of these rich whiz kids don't.

Jack and Sandy make predictable profits. A lot of these kids don't.

But the whiz kids are kicking the can. And the Cocoon Corporate crowd's gotta be wondering, "Wouldn't it be nice? Just for a day?"

# InterNOT!

### December 16, 1999

I think I know the hidden problem with a lot of these Internet stocks. It's not their prices, which by almost anyone's math are outrageous. Or their promise, which to almost anyone's reckoning is huge. No, it's their service—or, more to the point, their lack of service.

It's never more glaring than during the holiday season. To be fair, a lot of these e-commerce guys are deluged. So many are shopping online by pointing and clicking that many of the sites just can't handle it.

To a point, I can understand. But only to a point.

Now, I don't want to invite lawsuits here, so I'll keep specific names out. But let me pass on some experiences.

Take this one site that assured me weeks ago that a gift I was buying for my wife was in stock and would be delivered by Christmas. Turns out it won't be delivered by Christmas. That kind reminder was sent to me via e-mail, which prompted me to call up and politely inquire what the hell was going on.

After going through an automated voicemail response system that had me pressing about seven hundred buttons on my phone over the course of fifteen minutes, a very terse woman told me, "You're out of luck, sir."

To which I said, "You're outta your mind." And, "You're a liar."

You and your ever-so-seducing site swore on your high-tech bible that I'd have what I want, when I want. And all you can tell me is point, click, and poof?!

I don't think so. You see, that's the problem with some of these guys—and I stress *some*, because I really think most of 'em are okay.

In the pursuit of a quick buck, some are taking a few quick turns, and making quick enemies.

Retail Lesson 101, you high-tech idiots: the customers you tick off today are the ones you're losing tomorrow. I won't forget who's been good. And I sure as heck won't forget who's been bad. Because I have a very good memory, and right now a very short fuse. And like Santa, I'm making a list. But unlike you, Miss You're Out of Luck, Sir, I am checking it twice. So go stick that in your stocking.

# Out of Africa . . . Hope

*August 7, 1998*

It is easy to take a look at today's twin bombings in Kenya and Tanzania and conclude: It just ain't worth it. Why go there? Why invest there? Why even bother there?

Never mind that Africa has proven to be a resilient investment opportunity. Or that its masses, long mired in poverty, have made tremendous inroads to right their ways. Or that scores of American companies from Coca-Cola to Dunn & Bradstreet have set up shop on the continent. Or that President Clinton himself toured the region a few months back—something unthinkable years ago because of perceived security risks.

Big security risks right now. Uganda's under armed guard. Mozambique's under high alert. All true. All real. All frightening.

But do consider this: Mozambique's economy is growing in excess of 10 percent a year. South Africa now attracts capital from every major nation on this planet. And even the sites of today's deadly attacks—Kenya and Tanzania—have made great strides privatizing their industry.

It is not always easy. Or peaceful. Or bumpless. But it is the inimitable mark of progress. Sort of like investing in Germany before the Marshall Plan, or betting on France before Franco, or banking on Israeli companies when the Jewish state just began. Opportunities early. Rewards later.

Not always, and rightly unthinkable now. But worth considering down the road.

# I-M-F . . . U?

*January 7, 1998*

Be careful when you lend, because eventually you'll have to bend. That pretty much sums up the predicament of the International Monetary Fund and scores of global bankers, who've footed upwards of a hundred billion dollars' worth of emergency loans to places like Indonesia and Thailand and South Korea.

The unprecedented sums of money were given largely in the belief that it was as good for the lender as for the borrower. After all, as Donald Trump proved, you can't be too big, too important, not to fail. We didn't want Asia failing. We did, and do, a lot of business there.

But sometimes you gotta wonder who controls the chits.

Along comes Thailand to say it's not so sure it can repay the $17 billion we gave 'em . . . at least not on our terms. And then Indonesia sets a budget that is anything but austere. And now everyone wants to renegotiate. So what do we do?

Right now, we officially try to encourage them to change. They unofficially are telling us to kiss off. Now . . . who owes whom?

# Be Careful What You Wish For

*November 18, 1997*

What's that old saying. . . . Be careful what you wish for, because you just might get it.

Take America Online. Only a day after trumpeting its ten millionth customer, amid assurances that its worst problems were in the past, another fiasco hits.

This one concerns e-mail. For a while today, AOL subscribers couldn't get their e-mail. What's worse, they couldn't send their e-mail. An unspecified snafu, we were told. By mid-afternoon, customers were finally able to get their e-mail, but returning it was still a problem for some.

Problems happen, of course. And sometimes, they happen a lot. And in the case of AOL, being the biggest and baddest player in the online world, they get a lot of attention.

Some are already saying it's proof positive that AOL is growing way too fast, nabbing more subscribers than it could adequately service.

Maybe. Maybe not. But the timing couldn't be worse. What's that other expression. . . . The best of times, the worst of times.

# The New Thrilla in Manila

*August 8, 1997*

Hey, do you remember the third Ali-Frazier bout? The Thrilla in Manila?

It was a classic. Ali starts out strong, then it's Frazier, then Ali bounces back and takes a 14th round technical knockout.

Bear with me, I do have a point here, and in a word, it's this: economy. It's kind of like that Thrilla in Manila. Little more than a few statistics ago, the economy was described as softening, slowing, stabilizing. And that after being branded blistering, booming, burning.

Don't look now, but it's taking off again. Never mind that it's just a mild takeoff, economists like Dean Witter's Bill Sullivan tell me they see more activity in chain-store sales, some auto sales, and in factory production data.

That's what worries Wall Street. These guys fear that the economy's heating up too. I say "fear" because that likely means higher interest rates (it did today) and lower stock prices (it did today).

One day does not a trend make. But it does provide us with a snapshot, just like that Thrilla in Manila. A chance to catch an epic battle, yet again.

## Why My Daughter Should Be on the Fed

*December 5, 1996*

I don't often like to bring the musings of my eleven-year-old daughter onto a high-brow business show like this, but please indulge me.

The Federal Reserve's Lawrence Lindsey got me thinking of it today. Yeah, the Fed . . . my daughter . . . and Larry Lindsey.

You see, Mr. Lindsey was telling a group today that we're in debt. In fact, we're in debt a lot. And to quote him, "For every one dollar we are earning, we're spending $1.10. And this is not a sustainable trend."

Wow. To quote my daughter: "Duh."

I mean, this isn't exactly earth-shattering news. We've known about this debt problem for some time. We've known that consumers have racked up about a trillion dollars worth of red ink. We've known that debt loads are the highest they've ever been, period.

All true enough, but true for some time. Mr. Lindsey's been bemoaning it for some time.

But for all those warnings of financial Armageddon, still we wait. We've continued spending, because spending, frankly, is easier to do. Credit terms are more flexible. Interest rates are declining. And a lot of folks' total worth, thanks to a stronger stock market, has improved.

Sometimes you just need an eleven-year-old's perspective to put things into perspective.

## Why Bill Gates Matters

*November 25, 1996*

If you build a platform, you can leap. The question for one William Gates is whether his platform will be the one from which we all leap into the next century.

Rivals like Oracle System, Netscape Communications, and Sun Microsystems argue that Gates's Microsoft is today's hero, but not tomorrow's. They're all making the case for a stripped PC that gets what it needs via the

Internet, and not the traditional software venue that Microsoft dominates.

In a one-on-one interview, Gates tells me that individuals and businesses have spent far too much time, effort, and money investing in traditional technology. "Stick around," he tells them, "That technology is going to the next level via something called a Net-PC. It's a lot like a dumb box," Gates says, but smarter, much smarter. And more intuitive. More like the way we think.

It's too early to say that Gates has got it and others have not. But many a business has been foiled and fooled by underestimating the resourcefulness of this uncanny billionaire. Few are willing to risk being fooled again.


# Try This, Goldilocks

*November 15, 1996*

You keep hearing all this talk that what's really propelling this market to one record after another is a Goldilocks economy. A not-too-strong, not-too-weak, kind of recovery that keeps inflation in check and corporate earnings on the march.

The latest numbers bear out what we've been seeing for some time. In October, industrial production fell half a percent. It was the first drop in seven months. Meanwhile, something else called "capacity utilization" dipped as well. That's supposed to tell us how much of the factory floor is being used these days. And according to the latest statistics, it's not as much as before—down to 82.7 percent from 83.4 percent. Not a tumult, mind you, but a moderate fall.

Ditto you and me. Consumer confidence surveys say we're upbeat. But we're not giddy.

This is hardly the stuff of which reckless buying rampages are made. Hence, no need to worry about runaway inflation as consumer demand outpaces available supply.

Without sounding like some number-crunching economist, what it all means is this: things are stable, and the markets clearly expect them to remain that way.

Goldilocks. She did eventually run into some bears. But even then, she managed to run away.

Stay tuned.

# CHAPTER 19

# *BEING WRONG*

*I* told you I'd get around to the tough part—admitting when I
was wrong. I was just hoping that by burying it so deep into
the book you'd never get around to it. But in reality, I learned just
as much as my viewers and readers looking back at recent history—be it market or political history.

I correctly saw overheated markets, but I often ignored sometimes overheated individual stocks. Perhaps I was intrigued by the
company's story or, more to the point, the chief executive's story.
But whatever the excuse, this chapter includes the beauts I missed.

## Hot . . . on Hype

### October 30, 1996

Remember a little more than a year ago at this time, when all
those Internet initial public offerings were hitting the market?
And all that hype?

Scores of World Wide Web wannabes, debuting on Wall
Street with market values into the billions of dollars, had yet
to make so much as a penny. They were hot. Netscape. Lycos.
Secure Computing. Yahoo. All the rage.

And all a problem for a fellow named Bill Gates, who runs a company called Microsoft. Gates dismissed the Internet rage, all but calling it a high-tech flash in the pan. And, for quite a while, he looked right.

But even Mr. Gates eventually recognized that he might have been premature. So, better late than never, he crashed the Internet party with his own Web browser, called Explorer. And only this week he figured maybe all this stripped-down PC talk about a cheap machine able to download needed software, was worth exploring.

And only today, he predicted that the number of consumers on the World Wide Web will likely triple to 48 million by the year 2000.

Which is all a longwinded way of saying that maybe the hype was worth it. And that maybe, though premature, the profit potential was and is there.

## Krispy Kreme of the Crop

*April 6, 2000*

Leave it to a donut-maker to see through the hole in this market. Because, after all the hand-wringing on this volatile week in the markets, after all the Tuesday tumult, and tech wrecks, and B-to-be-gones, . . . after all that, I credit this turnaround not to a woman named Abby, but a company called Krispy.

I'm talking, of course, about Krispy Kreme, the donut folks who've gained a cult following on Main Street, and this week, a lot of respect on Wall Street, darn close to doubling in a debut many thought, at best, ill-timed.

After all, Krispy Kreme didn't have to go public this week. Advisers even suggested that the market tumult in the Nasdaq would have more than justified putting things on the back fryalator, so to speak. That there would be other days to make, umm, *dough*. Sweet profits could be had in calmer times.

But the captains of Krispy thought better. We're donuts, not dot-coms, dammit. Full steam ahead.

Nothing seizes the sweet smell of success better than a company that makes sweet things, and sweet money.

What motivated Metropolitan Life to go through with its initial public offering the very same day was the same thing that motivated Krispy Kreme. True, they don't make donuts, but they do make dough. And they do have guts. And together they both made believers out of tons of market doubters.

It is fitting that it took guys in a relatively boring, mundane businesses to bring us back to our senses. To make us recognize what all too many in-and-out day traders have forgotten: that good companies, with good plans, can still prove to be good bets. That's why it took a company named Krispy to turn around a market that looks grizzly.

Wall Street's still a scary place this week. But thanks to Krispy, it's at least looking a little more like a place of milk and honey. In more ways than one.

## The Good Lord, the Good Market

*January 10, 2000*

I always remember that story of the young Catholic priest who ran an orphanage back in the early 1900s, happily taking money from the notorious gangster Al Capone to run the place.

"I don't ask where it came from," he said, "because I know where it's going." And he added, tersely, "His money's just as good as anyone else's."

I think the good Father was right, and all the more so in light of America Online's stunning $350 billion pairing with Time Warner.

Critics say Internet money isn't real, and that even those who do make money, like AOL, don't make nearly enough to justify their lofty stock prices.

Maybe so, but who's to argue with an all-stock bid for which AOL is more than capable of footing the bill?

As another expression goes, their money is just as green as anyone else's. Who cares if the currency might be fleeting? It's real now. And its potential for tomorrow is enormous.

Deep down inside, I think a lot of these Internet kazillionaires sense they're sitting on a house of cards . . . some more sturdy than others. But they know a point-and-click empire doesn't make sense—not one that's valued dozens of times north of established brick and mortar institutions.

That's why I think a lot of 'em are compelled to do deals now, and to spend that currency now. After all, you never know if you'll have it down the road.

So I wouldn't be at all surprised to see a Yahoo or a CMGI strike while the deal-making iron is hot. Not because they want to. But, given the enormity of their latest transaction, maybe because they have to . . . while they still have it.

## Is the Euro a Zero?

*May 28, 1999*

If the euro's a zero, should we care-o?

I don't mean to be flip, but a lot is at stake here. In case you haven't heard, Europe's vaunted single currency is reeling right now, barely trading at parity with the dollar, down nearly 20 percent in the last few months.

This really isn't very complicated, though its implications are. You see, right now Europe's overall economy is still struggling, especially in countries like Italy and Germany. By contrast, we're cruising in the U.S.-of-A.

It comes down to this: If you wanted to buy a currency based on the strength of the economy it represents, where would you go? Trust me, you don't have to be famed global investor George Soros to figure this one out. People are going to the dollar—or, at the very least, not going to the euro.

Great for the dollar short term, but I think a very big problem for us, long term. Here's why.

Let's say the weakness in the euro is telling us something: that Europe is struggling and will continue struggling for some time to come.

What does that say about U.S. multinationals that do business in Europe? In two words, not much.

If you're a 3M or an Eastman Kodak or a DuPont or a Caterpillar, a potentially lucrative market looks decidedly less so. Not good for those companies who've increasingly grown to rely on biz from abroad.

And might I add that a lot of those companies reside in an average called the Dow Jones Industrials. If their sales don't measure up, neither will their profits, and ultimately neither will their stock prices. Reason enough for us to worry that what rattles 'em over there, will rattle us over here.

## The Other Armstrong

*February 1, 1999*

I've mentioned this once or twice on this show, but I hate—and I mean really hate—negative people.

First of all, they bring me down. And second of all, they bring a lot of other people down with them.

It's not that I mind them being negative. It's that they're being negative around me. The way I figure it, we all get thrown some real zingers in life. Some fair. Some not so fair. It's how we deal with those zingers that defines us and shapes us.

Take C. Michael Armstrong. When he took over AT&T a couple of years ago, he had every reason to feel like the cruise director on the Titanic. But where others found pity, he saw potential. And lots of it.

So he brought the company into cable by buying Telecommunications, Inc., and into the Internet by inheriting the speedy Web player, At-Home, and into our living rooms by hooking up with Time Warner.

He also vowed to cut jobs at AT&T, but not its heart. And he never demanded of those workers what he wasn't determined to do himself. Never bragging. Never shouting. Never waiting for others to implement what he himself couldn't deliver.

His boosters will say that's why AT&T is stronger than ever, why its stock price is higher than ever. Me? I think it's because he's happier than ever. Not so much because he's so upbeat now, but because he was just this way two years ago when others were not.

# Y2K Not OK

*August 19, 1998*

In case you didn't know, we are now officially 500 days away from the year 2000. That gives us 499 days to fix something called the Y2K problem.

You know all about that, don't ya? Computers around the world, capable of only reading the final two digits of any given year, will read 2000 as 1900, wiping out credit card records, social security records, defense records . . . you get the point. Lots of records.

To hear Deutsche Bank's Ed Yardeni tell it, Y2K could KO the economy, leading to a worldwide recession and such a costly fix-up that scores of businesses could be dragged under in the process.

I don't know if Ed's right. But I do know a lot of very smart folks that agree with him. Those who don't are almost cavalier in their dismissal, sure that it won't affect that many computers, or shut down that many airports and army movements.

Still, why take the chance? Major financial exchanges aren't. They've already run Year 2000 test drills to see how their computers would respond to the great turnover. And guess what. Their computers turned over.

They're ready. Sadly, most others are not. A big deal? Well, with five hundred days to go, would you take the chance to assume it's not?

# Bernie Ebbers . . . Genius

*October 15, 1997*

There's an expression on Wall Street that every dog has its day. That every loser is eventually loved. That stocks that look like poopers eventually become performers. It's the essence of bottom-fishing—finding those diamonds in the rough.

Enter one MCI. From darling to dog, and now back to darling.

Remember British Telecom's original $22 billion bid for the long distance company? Then, BT took a peek at MCI's books, saw some rough spots, and took it down a peg to $18 billion or so. And even then it looked like it was going to be ratcheted down, as MCI began to hemorrhage over more problems.

Enter Bernie Ebbers of WorldCom, who loved this so-called loser enough to plunk down more than $34 billion in stock for it. *In stock*. Today, reportedly in cash, there's another offer still—this one from GTE—willing to up the ante and confirm what we should have known all along: that this dog ain't a dog. And even if it is, it's having its day. And how.

## Long Live the Dollar

*October 18, 1996*

You've wanted a stronger dollar, you've got a stronger dollar. But what's that expression . . . be careful what you wish for?

I say that because that stronger dollar is starting to boomerang on the good old U.S.-of-A. It seems the stronger the dollar gets, the tougher it gets for U.S. manufacturers to sell their goods abroad.

You know how it goes. A strong dollar means it costs more yen for Japanese consumers to buy American cars. But it also hurts those same manufacturers here in the U.S. Foreign goods sell cheaply here. After all, Americans don't need as many dollars to buy Japanese products. Good for Nissan, Toyota, Sony, Nintendo, and on and on.

Any doubts? Just take a peek at that eye-popping $10.8 billion trade gap reported today for the month of August. Or that nearly $5 billion gap with China. Or a $3.7 billion imbalance with Japan.

The dollar's now trading at nearly a three-year high versus the yen. And that's prompted the big three automakers to essentially say *no mas.*

But for now there is no change. The dollar, reflecting our economy, looks like a good global investment bet. Good for the dollar. Not so good for the companies whose country it reflects.

# CHAPTER 20

# *ON DEATH AND DYING*

*D*uring my life I have given many eulogies—the most difficult being for my mother and father. But when someone asks me to do one, either for a relative or a friend or even an acquaintance, I readily agree. I figure it's the least I can do for the person who has departed this world. Because, when you come to think of it, the deceased are just running a bit ahead of the rest of us.

You might have noticed that I have a bit of a fixation with death. It strikes some as morbid, but to me it is as much a part of living as watching the day's news. After all, the very news I cover is fleeting. It passes in an instant. My bouts with illness no doubt fueled such somber analysis, but I also think it's part of my genetic makeup. I like to look beyond the here and now.

I see life and one's accomplishments as branded not in a moment, but in a lifetime of moments. We all make a mark on this planet for however briefly we're here. Some people make pretty big impressions, others decidedly smaller ones. But we all leave something behind. It's that something that I try to bring to a eulogy. When I look back at a life well lived, regardless of whose life it is I'm considering, I start with the premise that the person was flawed—but I end with the conclusion that he or she triumphed,

*despite and maybe even because of those flaws. It is why I refuse
to speak ill of the dead, or let others glom onto such potshots. The
dead are deserving of better. I try to find the room in my heart,
and on my show, to give them something better. They cannot fend
for themselves, or explain themselves, so I will try to do it—even
say it—for them.*

# Robert Atkins

### *February 13, 2004*

I want you to picture yourself dead. The coroner is confirming
you're dead. Weighing you. Measuring you. Then sliding you
into a refrigerator and saying goodbye to you, if you're lucky.

I want you to picture yourself being Robert Atkins.

The diet guru died last April. Rather than let him rest in
peace, though, a group that was long critical of the low-
carbohydrate diet he espoused is using his corpse to make a
point.

That group is called the Physicians' Committee for Responsible Medicine. It advocates vegetarianism. That's all well and
good. What's not good is what the group did to Robert Atkins.
Somehow, some way, they got their hands on Atkins' medical
records. Let me be blunt here: the crass details of a dead man
on a hospital gurney.

The group says Atkins was fat—258 pounds. Proof, one of
its members later told me, that Atkins either didn't practice
what he preached, or did and got fat anyway.

What the group failed to point out, and what *USA Today*
confirmed, is that Atkins went into the hospital weighing 195
pounds. He quickly fell into a coma, and lingered for nine days

in that vegetative state, being fed liquids that doctors tell me can, indeed, dramatically add weight in a short period. But what Atkins ultimately weighed going into and out of that hospital doesn't matter. Common decency does. And this Physicians' Committee for Responsible Medicine wouldn't know the first thing about it.

It's one thing to hate a diet. It's quite another to use a dead man to make your point about that diet. The dead man can't defend himself. So allow me.

I knew Atkins. I covered Atkins. The times I saw him, he didn't look obese to me. And why would he be? He was the poster child for the most talked-about diet revolution in human history! You don't stay on message if you're not staying in shape. And the Atkins I saw was staying in shape.

He freely told me that he'd battled weight in his life. It's a pity he can't battle classless fools in death.

The same fools who selectively cite only what they want in Atkins' medical records—who claim he had cardiomyopathy but forget to point out that it wasn't his diet that caused his heart ailment. It was a viral infection.

Look, I have no axe to grind on Atkins. I do have an ax to grind on fairness.

Try as critics might to disavow the health benefits of eating a low-carbohydrate diet, they can't. Most people who have done Atkins have lost weight, lowered their cholesterol, and lowered their blood pressure.

Now, some people don't *like* low-carb diets. That's fine. What isn't fine is condemning the success of those who have lost weight on it and have fitter physiques because of it.

The medical establishment never much flipped over Atkins when he was alive. They waited to pounce only when he was dead, and only then to use his corpse to make a point. These critics say the diet makes you sick. Right now, *they* make *me* sick—with their inconclusive studies, their unsupported claims, their high and mighty nutritional appeals. They think they've cornered the market on diets that work, but ignore the very real medical proof that the Atkins diet worked better.

I'm not saying they have to eat a steak to see the light. Just quit stabbing a stake through a dead man's heart to make a bloated point.

## Paul Tsongas

*January 20, 1997*

What with the inauguration and Martin Luther King Jr. Day, the passing of former senator Paul Tsongas over the weekend hasn't received a whole lot of coverage.

He had fought back recurring bouts of cancer and ultimately succumbed to pneumonia. But not before proving that illness needn't define the man or his mission.

You see, back in 1992, that mission for Tsongas was the White House. He wanted it, and briefly led the Democratic pack for it. But he was not your traditional Democrat.

He didn't want to alienate business. He welcomed it, with talk of economic incentives and capital gains tax cuts. And he blasted then-candidate Clinton's proposed middle-class tax cuts. "I'm not running for Santa Claus," he said at the time, "I'm running to be president."

He never got there. But he did go on to form the Concord Coalition with former Republican senator Warren Rudman to focus on the country's economic ills.

Throughout, Tsongas battled almost constant sickness. Constant pain. And almost constant rebukes from his own party. "No matter," Tsongas once told me, "It's time to make a difference." In his oh-so-brief fifty-five years on this planet, Mr. Tsongas can rest very much at peace . . . knowing he very much did that. And more.

# Diana

*September 2, 1997*

In a world of markets, indices, price earnings multiples, and currency valuations, Diana doesn't quite fit.

Never mind that Princess Diana had a lot of money, and was once part of a British royal family that had far more. No, to hear the British traders tell it, Diana was more than that.

She was a pretty savvy financier, as it turned out. Someone who uncannily looked after her financial interests when she was being heaved out on her royal derriere. She secured $22 million from the royal family, and an annual stipend of $600,000. What's more, she stayed a princess. How's that for a golden parachute?

Her thrust into the public eye covers a unique period in market lore as well. She appeared right before the global bull market in 1981 as a young princess. Full of promise. Full of hope. Like the markets, she had her ups and downs. But considerably more ups. Considerably more enthusiasts. Considerably more grateful for the experience of having known her.

No, Di is not a buy. She was a lot more than that. But she did personify our times—our best hopes, after our worst fears.

She was glitzy. And all were grateful for the chance to share her light. More than any trader. More than any market. More than any multiple.

She was bigger than that. And today, bigger. Much bigger still.

## John Chafee: Towering Senator from Tiny State

*October 25, 1999*

Sometimes you are judged not by the label people give you, but by the character you have inside you. I guess what's got me waxing poetic is the death this weekend of Rhode Island senator John Chafee.

For twenty-two years he represented the tiniest of states with the biggest of hearts and the most steadfast of missions. A Republican by name, he was not easily labeled conservative or liberal. Just as well, considering that he represented an overwhelmingly Democratic state.

But as a former resident of that state, I can tell you this: Rhode Islanders don't take easily to typical politicians. That's why they liked John Chafee. Not that they agreed with everything he did, but they liked the way he did it. With heart. With compassion. With a conscience. But, throughout, without an agenda.

He ended up losing a prominent Senate post in his party precisely because many party members thought he wasn't in sync with them on important issues. On the environment, for example, which he zealously sought to protect. And on health care, which he painstakingly strived to assure for all.

But just when Democrats thought they had one of their own in Grand Old Party clothing, Chafee was not above surprising them, too. He joined the filibuster against President Clinton's 1993 stimulus package, and years earlier supported George Bush's controversial nomination of Clarence Thomas to the Supreme Court. He stuck to his guns, even when it meant upsetting his state's powerful unions when he supported the North American Free Trade Agreement.

I don't care if you agree or disagree with Chafee on any or all of these issues. What you have to marvel at is that he took these stands . . . at great risk and great political peril.

As he reminded reporters, "I seek bipartisan solutions to problems rather than partisan gridlock."

Like I said, unusual.

My dad used to say, "I don't care if you're left-wing or right-wing, just be something. Believe in something."

Chafee did. And his tiny state is all the bigger for his efforts.

# Mother Teresa

### September 5, 1997

Mother Teresa died today.

Just announcing that on a business show says something about the kind of person Mother Teresa was. But don't think for a second that this remarkable woman didn't know how to work a corporate crowd.

It wasn't that she would strong-arm business to help her many causes to aid the poorest on this planet. I guess you would say she *inspired* them to.

I remember covering the fallout of the Bhopal, India, gas leak back in December 1984 at a Union Carbide plant. Two thousand people were killed. Union Carbide was criticized for dragging its feet—first for even acknowledging the gas leak was its own, and later, for getting help to the victims and families of victims involved.

Some shunned the area. Not Mother Teresa. Her presence prompted scores of others to intervene, including the Red Cross, and Catholic charities, and ultimately Union Carbide itself. "We want to do all we can," Union Carbide's chairman said at the time. Some say he was inspired by Mother Teresa's efforts.

She used to say that all people are inherently good, and that corporations are that way as well. "When you view them cynically," she said, "they will act that way." She didn't view them cynically. So, once she showed them how, they didn't act that way either.

A strong testament to a remarkable woman, and a pretty savvy one at that.

## Jordan's King Hussein

### February 5, 1999

It is probably blasphemous for me—a business anchor—to say this, but sometimes we think too much about money. How we make it. How we save it. How we cuddle it. And how we keep it.

What's got me thinking deeply here is the plight of Jordan's King Hussein. As you've no doubt heard, the sixty-three-year-old monarch has left the U.S. to go home to die. *To die.*

He had just spent nine days at Minnesota's famed Mayo Clinic, trying to fend off his aggressive non-Hodgkin's lymphoma. But after a last-ditch round of chemotherapy and bone marrow transplants, the king left as he entered . . . dying.

And I began to think. Here's a guy with all the money in the world. More money than you and me and all our friends, family, and acquaintances will ever see. A man who knew and befriended the most powerful people on this planet. Presidents and kings. Monarchs and mavens.

Yet with all that clout, all that influence, all that wealth, he is succumbing to the all-too-human condition we call "the end of the road."

Money and power and influence have given King Hussein so much in life. And he has given much back. But in the end, he simply wants to be home. Not with his money, but with his family. Because in the end, he figures—as should we—that the former is passing, but that the latter . . . is precious.

## Concorde

*July 25, 2000*

The Concorde.

The words itself bespeaks status. Luxury. A destination en route to a destination. And today, it bespeaks crash. The first in its stellar thirty-plus year history.

I don't know which will be remembered more.

Certainly for the next few days, at least, the latter. Not just because a plane crashed, but because *this* plane crashed. A plane taken by important people with important appointments to keep. CEOs and politicos, actors and actresses, the high and the mighty.

And for one couple, a month ago today, the not-so-mighty: Me and my wife.

In a reckless but sinfully enjoyable treat for her fortieth birthday, I decided to treat my wife to a weekend in Paris via the Concorde . . . *this* Concorde. This route. This day, a month ago, to the day.

It was not cheap. But it was memorable. Flying twice the speed of sound, this plane wasn't a ride, it was an event, one that afforded you a rare view of the arc of the earth itself from a perch higher than any other mere aircraft can reach.

But it was that, and much more. Unrivaled service. Impeccable food. And a clientele that compelled gawking, particularly for admittedly crass tourists like my wife and me. We saw chief executives and politicos, a famous talk show host and his model wife, and many more. We took it all in and marveled at this once-in-a-lifetime event.

And a fast trip at that, at little more than three hours or so to Paris—half the time a conventional plane would take. But somehow, all that speed, all that power, all that pizzazz seems to matter little now. My wife and I are grateful our trip had no problems.

The luck, or un-luck, of the draw, I guess.

I know I'm not being too profound here. But I guess I can't help thinking of the might-have-beens. I think of those who might have been flying this plane for the first time, filled with the same sense of awe.

None of this should take away from an appreciation for the fine things in life, as long as we don't forget that nothing is more important and more fleeting . . . than life itself.

## Victor Kiam

### May 28, 2001

You know, the fun thing about my job is interviewing a lot of interesting people.

One of my favorites died over the weekend: Victor Kiam. The guy who was so impressed with his Remington shaver that he bought the company. Victor was a character. And a controversial one at that. Just ask any New England Patriots fan and you'll get an earful about Victor, the team owner.

Victor never shied away from a good quote. He gave me plenty. He was tireless. He was energetic. And he was crazy. I say that in the fondest way. Who else would take a look at a money-losing U.S. shaver operation that was heading for certain bankruptcy and turn it around on sheer will? He was like a cheerleader, remembering even janitors by name, and birthdays and anniversaries of workers as if each were a CEO.

Maybe it was because Victor wasn't born rich that he never acted rich. I remember visiting his house in Connecticut for a profile I was doing. Our crew came early to set up. He was wandering around this unpretentious home in a bathrobe and kidding me that he looked better in that than a suit. Victor Kiam was not a suit. And not a man given easily to slowing down.

He joked about it with me a couple of years ago on this very set, after he had sold Remington. His wife was hoping he'd spend more time at home. She'd be disappointed.

Victor Kiam. Dead. At age seventy-four.

He will be missed.

## Alexandra Scott

### *August 13, 2004*

I read about it while I was away, far away. A little girl had died.

And I knew her. Talked to her. Had her on my show. She was all of eight years old. Her cancer-ravaged body, probably not even forty pounds, was weak. Frail. Tired. And dying. But even at this very table, she managed a smile. With her mom at her side, she spoke of wanting to help other kids fight the cancer that would all too soon conquer her.

Alexandra Scott.

An amazing little girl. With a big mission, that started with a little lemonade stand. To raise pennies, nickels, dimes, and quarters so that doctors might find a cure for what ailed her and so many others.

You know, it's amazing. After more than two decades interviewing the political and economic giants of this country, leave it to a frail, sickly, little girl to put them—and me—in perspective. I've talked to presidents and vice presidents, CEOs, actors, actresses, superstars of all stripes. But few touched me like little Alex. A girl wise beyond her years, stronger than her frail body suggested.

Some say we are defined in life by the big things we do. Sometimes I like to think we're also defined by how we die, and the little things we try to do. Alex was a small girl but a large human being. She's gone now. Her fight is over now. She is in better hands now. In a better place now. She deserves that dignity in death.

God knows she provided that much and more for all of us . . . in life.


## A Former President, a Wicked Hurricane, and a Lesson in Life

*September 7, 2004*

Money is nice. But it doesn't guarantee you'll avoid all things bad.

Take Bill Clinton. He has a lot of money. But it didn't prevent him from being hit with the same stuff that ails the rest of us—high cholesterol and highly clogged arteries. Or all those rich folks in West Palm Beach, Florida. Mansions without roofs. Everyone without power. Timely reminders, as if we need them, that money gets you a lot in life, but it doesn't shield you from the realities of life. Like heart attacks. Like hurricanes.

Mother Nature, I think, is the great equalizer. Foolish are the rich who refuse to see it. Or who think their money shields them from it. There is nothing so humbling as seeing your home destroyed and everything you know gone. There is nothing so terrifying as going under the knife for a condition all the money in the world can't prevent.

True, the rich are better able to rebuild, and maybe better able to afford top care. They might well live longer. Good thing. Because it's not as if they can take with them, in death, the things they so enjoyed in life.

## Dying with a Smile

*December 9, 2004*

I don't mean to close on a morbid note, but right now, I want you to think about dying. Dying soon. Let's say in a matter of months.

I mention this because I ran into someone who is facing this prospect. A fifty-two-year-old woman whose advanced cancer is apparently incurable. She's nixed treatments that could extend her life, at best, by a matter of months. So she wants to go out, she tells me, with dignity.

But not before enjoying one last meaningful Christmas with her family. She's hosting. And cooking. And shopping.

And everyone is coming. Far from being devastated, she couldn't be happier. "We all gotta go," she tells me. "I just have a better idea when."

She's a woman of deep faith. I met her as she was coming out of New York's St. Patrick's Cathedral. She recognized me. Seemed eager to talk to me. Said she liked my show. Had a message for me. "Keep talking money," she said. "But don't forget the other stuff, the important stuff."

She joked about telling her kids, "No gifts for me this year. Don't have much time to use them."

"So what do you want this season?" I ask her.

"Them," she said. "One last time."

We parted ways with me thinking what I would do if I knew this Christmas would be my last. Would I be so brave? So focused? So selfless?

I don't know. But this day, this much I did know. I was running late to pick up a gift.

And, suddenly, I didn't really care about being late.

# Rhode Island Disco Fire

### *February 21, 2003*

The unexpected.

How often we are taken aback by things we never saw coming: A deadly fire in Rhode Island. A similar disaster just four days earlier in Chicago. The crash of the shuttle *Columbia* just two weeks before that.

So many numbing events in so little time. They seem to happen so fast, it's as if we can't catch our breath before we catch the next horror, the next shocker, the next nightmare.

Maybe it's just me, but we used to be able to space these things out. I can remember months of soul-searching after the *Challenger* blew up. I covered that story, and it seemed to linger longer.

Not *Columbia*. No sooner were we grasping the dimensions of that calamity than we were onto another one . . . war. And then heightened terror alerts. And then blizzards. And then nightclub fires. Unexpected. But at a pace that seems all too expected. All this, a byproduct of the post-September 11 world, where we fear the worst, and happily settle if things just get a little worse.

I heard one parent in Rhode Island talking about how she was frantically looking for her son after hearing of the fire. She found him, thank God, and said, "I just hugged him as tight as I could."

You just never know, she said.

No you don't. But you do appreciate that loved one as you're trying to figure it all out. And you hug . . . even tighter.

# John Ritter

*September 12, 2003*

How many of us are ticking time bombs?

The reason I ask is the death of actor John Ritter. He was only fifty-four, and apparently succumbed to something he didn't even know he had—a flaw in his heart, a dissection of the aorta.

It got me thinking: What's inside us that could kill us?

The Heart Association puts out warnings for heart attacks. There are signs you can look for if you're worried about a variety of cancers. But hidden dangers, dangers like those that claimed the life of Mr. Ritter, well, for those there are few, if any, signs.

Medical experts say that an examination could have revealed Mr. Ritter's deficiency. Others aren't so sure. We live in an age where almost anything we eat seems dangerous. And almost anything we touch seems risky. There are so many ways we can die.

Maybe it's a good thing a lot of us don't know until we do. It would be very easy to get paranoid, and easier still to turn into a hypochondriac. I just wish there were a tell-tale checklist of signs, or signals, or something that says, "Hey, look into this." Many women do. Most men do not. And so it goes. Living day-to-day with things that could kill us.

I know we'll all meet the same fate. I just wonder if, and how, we could put it off.


# Tsunami

### January 3, 2005

I don't think there is anything that so grips the living as images of the dead. The wrath of Mother Nature played out again and again on television screens across the globe, showing how 150,000 and counting lost their lives on this globe. I have little to add to all the coverage, save maybe this all too obvious point.

You just never know.

Think of all the thousands who visited these hot tourist spots, looking forward to sun and fun, whose survivors are now thinking only search and recovery. How quickly life changes—in an instant, from long-planned vacations to hastily planned funerals. In the proverbial blink of an eye. Tragic for the residents who lived there. Tragic for the vacationers who simply wanted to chill there.

I remember how Evil Knievel was asked about the peril of his mission when he attempted to cross the Snake River Canyon back in the 1970s. "If it doesn't work out," he said, "I'll just be one step ahead of the rest of you."

Profound statement then. Profound statement now. We really don't know the time . . . or the place. The occasion . . . or the moment. We only know that it's coming. Reason enough for so many of us to stop thinking about it coming altogether.

So we focus on the next trip. The next family get-together. We save. We toil. We plan. And we hope.

Nothing good comes of tragedies like these, save the realization that at any time, anywhere, at any moment, what we cling to . . . goes.

Enough maybe to make us think more, hug more, do more. While we still can. While we're still here.

## Billy Crystal on Broadway

### *January 19, 2005*

So the other night, my wife and I caught comedian Billy Crystal's Broadway show, *700 Sundays*. Believe me, I'm no theater reviewer, so I won't play one now. But I have to tell ya, it's an amazing show.

In it, Crystal recounts the first fifteen years of his life—the roughly 700 Sundays he enjoyed innocently before his dad died of a heart attack. What struck me was Crystal's message in the very end. And I mean the very, very end. After all the laughter. And yes, all the tears. Crystal came out for the obligatory and much-deserved standing ovation.

In thanking everyone for coming, he harkened back to the characters and memorable family members he highlights in the show, most of whom are now long gone.

"We all have special people in our lives," he said. "Call them . . . while you still can."

It was simple. But powerful. How many of us wish we had our loved ones with us for just one more cup of coffee? One more laugh? One more meal around the table?

Time has a way of taking them from us.

Leave it to Crystal to crystallize not letting time take them so fast that we don't squeeze in a quick call—maybe several quick calls—before they're gone . . . forever.

# TWA Flight 800

*November 1, 1999*

For the longest time, we knew their story. We just didn't know their names. Until now, more than thirty-six hours after the crash.

The victims of Egypt Air Flight 990 were shrouded in the mystery of this inexplicable disaster. News organizations across the globe have been covering this story over and over, desperately seeking to find out who was on that plane. And while the journalist in me wants to know too, the person in me forces me to wait until families have all been notified . . . no matter how long it takes.

I know that sounds blasphemous, particularly for someone in my biz. But after interviewing scores of victims' families at times like these, I can tell you this: Their rights come long before mine. Their pain is far greater than mine. Their loss is far more piercing, their anger far more justified and palpable.

I remember talking last night with a guy who lost both his wife and his two daughters in that TWA Flight 800 crash a few years back. He's still angry, and rightly so, that authorities were quicker to talk to reporters at the time than to families.

Authorities this go-round are bending over backward trying not to repeat that mistake. So they waited. No names, at first, but lots of stories . . . of the senior citizen group taking off for a fourteen-day tour of Egypt . . . of the seventy-two-year-old woman celebrating her anniversary with the love of her life . . . of the mother and son reunited on a tour of the ancient civilization they studied for decades and saved for for years. They're all gone now.

Their families know their names. We know their stories. We all know their fate.

As it should be. More details will follow. But in due course.

Families first. Journalists like me second. Again . . . as it should be.

## MS

*September 3, 2002*

Speaking of attitude, I've been getting quite a bit of e-mail these last few days over a *People* magazine profile of me in its latest edition. Not all of it good.

Terry Ribicoff e-mails: "Why is it I have to read in *People* that you have multiple sclerosis and are a cancer survivor? I suffer from MS, and I am a nobody. You have this great platform and never use it to help the rest of us who suffer so much. You seem like a nice guy, Neil, but after reading this, I'm disappointed."

I'm sorry you feel that way, Terry. I don't think I hide from my MS. I mention it, when appropriate, like when I'm talking to the CEO of the company whose drugs I take to fight it. But that's it.

As I told *People*, I'm not a platform or a cause. The best way I can help people with this disease is to prove you can move on, despite this disease.

I've said it before. I'll say it again. We all bear our crosses in life. Some are heavier than others. Many are a lot heavier than mine. But I'd rather be defined by what I do, not by what I have. So why bloviate on what I have? And seeing as I appear to collect diseases, why should I be partial to one over another?

I'm an optimist at heart, Terry. And my optimistic way of helping those with disabilities is to prove to the world that we are greater than the sum of our disabilities. You can't preach that. You have to live that. I choose the latter.

You see, Terry, I firmly believe that you can take a stand . . . without standing on a soapbox.

## Dying, and Smiling

*December 8, 2003*

She is poorer than she was last year. Benefits that she's grown to depend on are running out this year. Her paralysis from a devastating neurological condition is worse this year. She looks older now. More feeble now. More vulnerable now.

But it's not until you talk to her that you realize she's not much different now. She's very excited about the holidays. Unable to shop in malls, she buys on the Internet. She can't afford much, so she doesn't buy much. But each gift is unique. Each gift actually is funny. One for a brother. Another for a friend. Both plan to join her this Christmas.

Her luxury is lattes. She says she's famous for them. And guests love them. A small treat, she adds. But it's not her lattes that keep her guests coming—or those gifts. It's her. Her warmth. Her determination. Her goodwill in the face of bad stuff.

I was introduced to her through an acquaintance—an acquaintance fairly sick himself. But he, like she, was sick in body only. Not soul.

I don't even remember her name. Only that she's going through a very tough spell this holiday season. And you wouldn't know it. Even if you asked.

## A School Shooting. Again.

*March 5, 2001*

Another school shooting. Sadly, sometimes, no matter how often you hear about it, you can't help but be fascinated by it. If you're a parent, feeling for the parents of these students in the latest shooting, all you can do is wish for the best and say, "There but for the grace of God, go I."

Right about now, you're likely wondering what a business news guy is doing commenting on a general news story like this. Here's what. Events like this put events like the ones I cover in perspective.

I mean, think about something for a moment. Do you think the parents of any of these kids, either those injured, or those just there, gave a lick about this market? Or the drubbing they've had in technology stocks? Or whether we're in a recession or just a slowdown?

No, I don't think any of that came to mind today. I think all of that stuff, for these parents at this moment, was and is noise. Just noise. Their kids, and whether they're all right—that's what mattered. That's what matters. And so it should.

Sometimes events like these are hard to cover—harder still to comprehend. But if any good comes out of them, it's this: You discover what's important. And what isn't.

You learn about what's priceless. And what just has a price. There is a difference. Especially for these parents.

It takes events like these and unexpected tragedies like plane crashes, floods, and hurricanes to separate what matters from what doesn't. You can lose money, but you can always get it back. You can be down on a stock, but you can always choose another stock. All that's fleeting stuff. Disturbing stuff, yes. Troubling stuff, most definitely.

But just stuff, in light of events like these.

So count your blessings, my friends, and remember that just when you think you have it bad . . . you could have it worse.

A lot worse.

## The Priceless Paul Allen

*November 15, 1999*

They say a serious illness gives you focus. So what if you have a serious illness and a lot of money? What does that give you? Well, to watch Microsoft cofounder Paul Allen, you'd think it gives you license to do pretty much whatever you want . . . whenever you want.

Allen was stricken with Hodgkin's disease, a sometimes devastating form of cancer, just as he and his buddy Bill Gates were really taking off. After a battery of chemotherapy and radiation that ultimately saved his life, Allen quit Microsoft. He could afford to. His stake in the software giant today is worth more than $40 billion . . . making him among the richest people on the planet.

But it's what Allen has decided to do with that money and himself that has made him a remarkable figure, even one in so-called retirement. He was and is an uncanny investor, and uses the freedom of being gainfully employed to make big gains in new technologies. His gut is as good as his bank account, whether it's betting early on the promise of cable, and making a huge payday for himself with the public offering last week of his Charter Communications, or sensing the lucrative potential for Internet travel sites, by indirectly profiting off Microsoft's online Expedia service, or doubling his net worth by scoring big with his nearly five million-share stake in Web traffic organizer Internap Network Services.

But if that's all there was to Allen, he'd go down as nothing more than a shrewd businessman. He has set up charitable foundations that attack diseases as diverse as cancer and AIDS, and has contributed to causes as big as illiteracy and substance abuse.

He doesn't have to do any of this. He could, as they say, sit back, sip a margarita, and watch the boats go by. But I guess having flirted with death, Paul Allen wants to get the most out of life—as an investor, and, apparently, as a human being. Reason enough that some who have flirted with the reaper insist they are richer for the experience.

# JFK Jr.

*July 26, 1999*

I like to think that on a show like this, business news is important, but that it isn't all-important. I mean, being rich is nice, but being alive is better.

Just ask John Kennedy Jr., his wife, and her sister. You see, from even where I was vacationing in the Canadian Rockies, it didn't take too long for our friends north of the border to feel the futility of all this south of the border. All the Kennedy wealth. All the Kennedy influence. And money. And good looks couldn't save John Junior from a fate all of us, rich or poor, will eventually face. That's the tough part. The sad part.

But it isn't the only part. Just ask Lance Armstrong, winner of this year's Tour de France. Only a few years ago, he was all but given up for dead. Testicular cancer had spread to his lungs and brain. Many had lost hope for Lance. But not Lance. "The reaper will come," he said, lying in his Indiana hospital bed, dizzily enduring round after round of debilitating chemotherapy, "But not now. Not yet." There were races to win. And mountains to climb.

Armstrong's victory comes not a moment too soon for all of us. Because just like an Armstrong of another era, this one wanted to leap to new highs, even as our national psyche was driven to new lows.

Sadly, we will remember JFK Jr., for the might-have-beens for the tragedy of his death. Lance Armstrong put our focus, properly so, on the promise of life. It is short. It is fleeting. It is neither quarter to quarter, nor year to year. It is day-to-day. Lance taught us to appreciate the promise of life, while we have it, while we hold it, while we enjoy it, and hopefully, all, before we inevitably lose it.

No, you can't take it to the bank. But you can take it . . . to heart.

# Give the Dying a Chance

*March 23, 2000*

Let me ask you something. Do you have a serious disease or know someone who does?

Let's say you do. You'd probably do almost anything to help yourself if you could. Especially if the alternative isn't good. If the disease in question cripples you. Or kills you. It could compel you to do something, anything, to improve your odds. And I think it was that thinking that got the Food and Drug Administration to start approving drugs more quickly.

The idea was, and is, that people badly need these drugs. And regardless of their side effects, they've still got to be better than the ravaging effects of the disease they're attacking. I remember one terminally ill cancer patient testifying before Congress saying, "What do I care if an experimental drug might kill me? I'm going to die anyway." Good point.

But what if the disease isn't going to kill you, but the drug just might? Different story, right?

Now you have the bullet points on Rezulin. That's the diabetes drug that Warner-Lambert just pulled off the market, after reports that some patients were dying after taking it. More than sixty, at last count. To be fair, this is but a fraction of the more than half-million who benefited from it.

But sixty-three people dying of liver failure because of Rezulin does raise serious questions. For example, is the cure worse than the disease? Especially when the disease is far from fatal when kept in check.

To be sure, Rezulin has its benefits. It's one of a promising new breed of drugs that helps diabetes patients stop resisting insulin. But other drug makers have products on the market that do similar things.

So what was the rush? Authorities say Rezulin wasn't rushed to the market at all, and that risks are associated with all treatments. I agree. As long as we don't go slow with all drugs for all diseases.

Because while some treatments are risky, a lot of diseases are fatal. Some patients just weigh their odds. And that's their choice. Their risk. Take a chance, or take a pass on life.

What would you do?

# CHAPTER 21

# . . . AND DEPTH

*I*'ve long held to the view that the overwhelming majority of us *are good people, caring people, decent people—people trying to get by and do whatever good we can for our kids, our family, and our friends. Some of us succeed beyond measure. Others need to be reminded of that measure. And I'm not talking about the typical measuring sticks we use to gauge our lives on earth. I mean the principles valued by a much higher power, far from this earth. It's the small, lasting, priceless values that lend depth to our daily lives.*

## A Kidney for a Coworker

*February 17, 2000*

Let me ask you something. Would you give a kidney to a coworker?

Don't laugh. That's exactly what Laura Montoya did for Mary Kirby, a customer service representative at Comcast Cable.

Imagine that. A kidney . . . to someone you don't even know that well. But as Laura told Stephanie Armour in a wonderfully uplifting page-one story in today's *USA Today,* Mary Kirby was hurting. Bad. She was in dialysis. Medication wasn't helping. In short, Mary was dying, quite literally, to get a kidney.

So Laura came to Mary with an offer: Take one of mine.

Mary's generous act of kindness wasn't unique. Armour writes of forty-six-year-old Cindy Scimemi, who pained for thirty-year-old Steven Schibetta, ravaged with kidney disease. She gave him hers. Or of Nancy Nearing, who gave a kidney to her boss. Her boss! Would you do that? For your boss?

There are a lot of other stories just like that. People who do really big things for people they don't really big-time know. Not because they have to, but because they want to. As that forty-six-year-old donor mom put it, "I didn't save his life. God did that. I just provided a tool for someone else to make his life better."

That's one amazing lady. And even more amazing is that there are so many like her. People doing extraordinary things in our very ordinary work world.

So the next time someone tells you about how cold and indifferent workers have become in this country, think of Cindy . . . and Nancy . . . and Laura. People with hearts so big, they'd give 'em away if they could—and if they had two, no doubt, they would.

## Fat Woman, Cruel World

*March 22, 2000*

It never ceases to amaze me how cruel some people can be. How, for no apparent reason, there are some on this planet who go out of their way to pick on others. Abuse others. Embarrass others.

Now I know what you're gonna say: *There goes Neil getting on his high horse again.* But bear with me. Because what has me stewing is a poignant piece in today's *New York Times* about a woman named Lynnda Collins, who can't seem to find full-time work.

It's not that she's not talented. It's just that she's fat. And not just a little fat. Nearly half the adults in this country are a little fat. No, Lynnda is really fat. She weighs in at 325 pounds and stands only five foot six.

Go ahead, snicker. Lynnda hears it. Sees it. Feels it. But Lynnda's a person too. And from what I could read of her interview with reporter Micky Reece, she's a pretty nice person at that.

Fretting over a crucial job interview, she says, "I try to be hopeful. But I go through spells when I'm hopeless and I cry a lot."

Things haven't been easy for Lynnda since she lost her job after thirteen years of working for a company called GEAC Computer. The company says Lynnda was just one of many workers in its Atlanta office it had to lay off. Downsizing. It's happening to everyone.

Lynnda isn't so sure. She wonders whether her appearance has anything to do with it. Apparently her résumé is great, and she has no problem getting interviews. It's just that once she shows up, her fortunes head down.

Maybe some companies fear the medical issues. And maybe for good reason—obesity can lead to lots of other bad things. But somehow taking 'em out on Lynnda seems to me an even worse thing. Because it's not a racial thing or a quota thing. To me, it's a far nastier thing.

And I don't think it should be. Not because I'm a little big, but because so many others have to be so damn small . . . on the inside.

## What Al Gore Could Learn from Joe Lieberman

*December 9, 2003*

You know who I feel sorry for right now? Joe Lieberman.

Imagine being this guy. He holds off entering the 2004 presidential race until he knows for sure that his old running mate pal, Al Gore, isn't joining the contest.

Everywhere he goes, Joe says nice things about Al. How he was robbed. How he was cheated. How he was a good man who got a raw deal. You might not agree with Joe politically, but you can't deny the fact he was good and decent to Al Gore personally.

Then what does Al do? He zings him. Big time. Not only endorses Howard Dean for the Democratic nomination, but doesn't have the common decency to call Joe up and tell him.

How difficult would that call have been to make? Something like, "Hi, Joe, it's Al. Got some bad news for you. No offense, but your campaign doesn't appear to be going anywhere. Dean seems to be the guy. So I'm hopping on that bandwagon and keeping my options open . . . *Capiche*?" Actually, never in a hundred years would you hear Al Gore say *capiche*, but you get my point. It still would have been slimy and phony and wormy. But it shouldn't have been *as* slimy or *as* phony or *as* wormy.

No matter. Al's with How. And Joe's with nobody. There's no reward for loyalty in life. There's less of it in politics. Just ask Joe.

# Groping to Make a Point

*October 3, 2003*

A lot of people ask me about bias in the media. I always have a standard response: The issue isn't what the media reports, it's what the media does not report.

For example, I think it's fair game to report these fondling allegations about Arnold Schwarzenegger. What's odd is why they weren't brought up earlier, especially considering that the *Los Angeles Times* was sitting on the story much, much earlier.

I think it's fair to question a gubernatorial candidate's commitment to women if he has a raucous past with some women. What's odd is not bringing up the same about a former president who had a lot of experiences with a lot of women, before and even while he was president.

I think it's fair, though a little weird, to dig up decades-old comments a candidate made about Adolf Hitler. What's odd is not creating nearly the same fuss when a senator named Byrd used the "n" word on a national television show.

I think it's fair to call groping what it is—wrong and unacceptable—when it involves a man called Schwarzenegger. What's odd is ignoring Juanita Broaddrick's allegations of something far more serious involving a man named Clinton.

And I think it's fair for NOW and other women's groups to come out and attack Schwarzenegger over his views on women. What's odd is how none of them said *boo* when it involved Bill Clinton.

I ask: Why are the same folks who argued that sex shouldn't be an issue when it involved a Democrat, now creating such a stink when it involves a Republican?

Perhaps because they're hypocritical, phony, smarmy worms with an agenda as transparent as their own puffed-up egos.

I'll report. Please . . . you decide.

## The Whiner at the Cocktail Party

*September 5, 2003*

Tell me if this has ever happened to you. You're at an event and you get stuck talking to someone you'd rather not get stuck talking to.

I like almost everybody. My wife says that's because I'm hopelessly naïve. There are exceptions though: negative people. I really lose patience with people who complain. And whine. And carp. . . . Exactly what I'm doing now, going on about them!

But seriously, the other day I was next to this woman who seemed to know a lot about me personally. And the subject of illnesses came up. I'm sympathetic to such issues, since I'm pretty aware of such issues. But my point is, this woman wouldn't stop talking about how everyone was out to get her.

She seemed to have a fairly minor ailment, but Oh my God, the boss doesn't sympathize with her. The kids don't call her. The neighbors don't even bother to contact her. I nodded my head, desperately looking for the drink guy, but she was just warming up. She tells me her feet swell, and that her podiatrist is a jerk. That her kitchen's falling apart, but where on earth could you find an honest contractor? And so on.

I'm sure she was a good person, but she clearly didn't have a good word to say about anyone or anything.

Into my third glass of wine, I finally got up the gumption to say, "Surely something good is going on in your life."

She stopped, thought, and just when I thought she was about to say something positively profound, she ranted about her grandkids, whose parents apparently rarely allow her to see.

I wonder why.

She asked me what she should do. Dizzy now, I thought, "Shoot yourself!" But I said, "Get a hold of yourself. You've got a lot of baggage. But you look like you can carry it . . . consider yourself lucky. And look at the alternative. You could be dead."

She gave me a quizzical look, then moved on.

And I had . . . one more drink.

## Two Weeks, Two Lifetimes

*May 19, 2003*

I'm a bit of a pack rat—I even save newspapers. This past weekend I stumbled on a paper that was fairly recent, just two weeks old, and I was amazed to see all that's happened in those two weeks.

There was a report that the Senate Finance Committee would likely include none of the president's dividend-tax cuts. It ended up including virtually all of them.

Another piece was on how al Qaeda had been humbled—unable to launch attacks. Before Riyadh. And Morocco. And more than fifty were killed in al Qaeda attacks.

Still another story talked about the unusual quiet breaking out in the Middle East ahead of Colin Powell's reported trip to the region. Two weeks later, half a dozen attacks would claim dozens of lives.

In corporate news, AOL's Steve Case was reported as "virtually certain" not to get reappointed to AOL's board. The report was wrong. Case was reappointed.

SARS was scaring everyone. It still is.

The Yankees were on top of the baseball world, with no one in sight. They're still on top, but the Boston Red Sox are now not only within sight, they're tied.

A columnist talked of bonds getting pricey, and how interest rates couldn't go lower. Two weeks later, they're pricier still, and rates are nearly a quarter percent lower.

UAL was reported on life support. Two weeks later it was hiring back workers.

People on the ropes then . . . coming back now.

People very much alive then . . . very much dead now.

Leave it to an old newspaper to tell us where we were, and to tell us how mightily we've screwed up since. It makes me wonder what I'll be reading two weeks from now. Or two days from now. Or maybe seeing only two hours from now.

Lesson learned: The things we think are certain often are not. The things we think are unlikely often are.

My father used to say a good day is reading the obituaries and seeing you're not among the names listed. He last said that about a month before he was among those names listed.

Things changed. I just wish they wouldn't change . . . so quickly.

## Time to Look at Time

*April 5, 2004*

I know I've mentioned this on the show before, but the whole issue of time amazes me. How it passes. How it changes. How it . . . humbles. I mean you can be on top of the world one minute, then with nothing the next.

What's got me waxing poetic is a chance meeting I had with a Texas bigwig while I was away last week. There was a time when this guy was the "it" guy, often quoted, often praised, often the subject of page one headlines.

But that was then. This is now. And now, he's retired— from jetsetter to jilted in what seems like the blink of an eye.

I bumped into him the very same day I heard that the folks at Dow Jones were kicking some venerable names out of their exclusive Industrials club. AT&T, International Paper, and Eastman Kodak are out. Pfizer, AIG, and Verizon are in. They make their Dow 30 debut this week. The others march off the stage just to make room.

I can remember the days when AT&T was the greatest company on earth. Its stock was so highly regarded that it was considered the safe haven for widows and orphans. Now, *it's* the one orphaned from the financial world, the cool Dow Jones Industrials world.

It happens. It's called time.

It's the same cruel commodity that takes an Eastman Kodak from being a photography giant to a digital dunce. Just like that, the "it" guys are no longer "it"; are no longer in the club; no longer get the invites or the attention. They go from standouts, to don't let the screen door hit you on the way out. . . .

Kinda hard to figure out.

It's a timely reminder, as if any of us need it, that we should relish the good times when we have them. And never assume, not for a minute, that there is any guarantee we shall always have them.

It's why I think good press is nice . . . but a good perspective is nicer still.

## What the Little Guy Could Teach the Big Guy

*August 8, 2000*

I might have told you about this investment seminar I was at some time back. I was moderating a discussion among invest-ment pros about how they play the market. One knucklehead on the panel says, "However, the little guy doesn't play the market."

He couldn't have been more arrogant. Or condescending. He made it abundantly clear how little he thought of the little guy. I found it pretty dumb at the time, and I told him as much, especially since the audience we were addressing was made up of "little guys."

I hated him and his elitist view. And, to be fair, he hated me. He said I set out to roast him on the panel. Perhaps I did . . . but he started it!

How's that for maturity?!

The whole reason I'm bringing this up is that some in the financial community—blessedly not all, but some—seem to think they have all the answers, and that the rest of us have all the ignorant questions.

But I have another view. I think average folks are pretty smart. And I'll take their common sense over the other guys' Ivy League book sense any day, anywhere, anytime.

Here's why: They ain't rocket scientists.

Look at this guy Henry Blodgett. He's now become a media superstar because of something he foresaw sometime back—that Amazon.com would rocket to $400 a share. It did soar. And so did Henry. He's Merrill Lynch's wunderkind Web watcher. His musings are darn near Delphi-like. So when he decided to downgrade eleven of some twenty-nine Web stocks he follows, Wall Street took notice, and investors took sell orders.

But wait a minute. Prices had already tumbled for a lot of these guys. Pets.com and Buy.com were already selling at a fraction of what they once were. It made me think that panning these issues was sort of like closing the barn door after all the animals had escaped. Methinks there's still a foul smell in that barn—not from the jackass who ran out, but from the jackass who's still in.

Either way, the whole thing stinks. Because those guys aren't that smart. And we aren't that dumb. They know that. They just hope we don't.

## Dull Is Sexy

*July 27, 2000*

Is being dull a handicap?

The reason I ask is that a lot of people are making a lot of fuss over Dick Cheney, George W. Bush's vice presidential pick. "Unexciting," says the *Washington Post*. "Corporate," says the *New York Times*. "Decidedly uncharismatic," rants *USA Today*.

Okay, so this former defense secretary and Halliburton CEO isn't tearing up the charisma meter. I say, who cares? I'm not here to judge the political wisdom in picking a Dick Cheney to be on a ticket. To be sure, he probably doesn't bring Mr. Bush a lot more votes. And unlike a John McCain or a Colin Powell, he doesn't draw in different voter blocks either.

So he's dull. I happen to like dull. For me, dull is okay in a vice president, and doubly okay in a president. I don't need to be awed and wowed. I don't even need a guy who sparkles on the stump. I say, enough with colorful characters. Give me boring. Because what they might lack in sparkle, they often more than make up for in substance.

Take accountants—in general, not a sexy lot. But generally, good at doing your taxes. Take band singers—great at weddings, but would you want them filing your taxes? I don't think so. Because, for certain jobs, at certain times, you'd much rather have the dull guy with little hair than the pizzazz guy with lots of it.

Don't get me wrong. A good president who has a good way with words can go a good long way toward inspiring folks. Ronald Reagan was a master at it. And even Bill Clinton's critics must admit that he gives one hell of a speech. It just disturbs me that in politics—and increasingly in business—we're putting a priority on the sizzle and forgetting that, in the end, it's the steak that we eat.

You know, they say Abraham Lincoln never would have been elected president today. A whiny voice, a deliberate, almost brooding manner. I don't know. But this much I do know: Charisma ain't all it's cracked up to be. Lincoln didn't have it. But I'm sure glad we had him.


## The Rich Are Cheaper Than You and Me

*February 22, 2000*

So you want to be a millionaire?

Well, if you can't get on the game show—or marry one—try this: Be frugal. Be determined. Be religious. And be loyal to your spouse.

Such are the findings of a fascinating book called *The Millionaire Mind,* by Thomas Stanley. He's the same guy behind the bestseller *The Millionaire Next Door,* a book that suggests the rich aren't very different from you and me—they just have a lot more money. But it's what they do with that money—or, rather, what they don't do—that's really revealing.

For one thing, they don't show off. Most of them don't have fancy cars, or ski the Rockies. Or take cruises around the world. Or jaunt off to Paris for the weekend.

Most of 'em work—hard. And that's because most of 'em are not exactly Einsteins. They got a 2.9 grade point average in school, scored under a thousand on their SATs, but are sweating like the dickens to prove they're better than that.

And oh yeah, they're frugal. No, let me be more specific. They're cheap. Cutting coupons. Reupholstering their furniture. Mending their clothes. Even making shopping lists! So the next time you eye that guy with the filled-to-the-rim cart at Costco, don't laugh. He could probably buy and sell ya.

. . . Which brings me back to my point. The one thing I learned from Stanley's two books on the subject is that the average millionaire is focused not only on what he has in the bank, but also on what he has at home. On average, a spouse of twenty-eight years. Twenty-eight years! He's a guy who would much rather spend time with his kids than with his shareholders.

He's rich all right. In many, many more ways than one.

## Opening Doors, and Hearts

*November 30, 2004*

He opens doors. Literally. And he smiles. A lot. He's a doorman. And his name is Tony. And no matter the season, or the weather, Tony's always the same. Always smiling. Always laughing. Always kidding.

No detail is too small for Tony. He takes particular interest in those visiting from out of town. Restaurants they should go to that won't cost 'em an arm and a leg. And the best time to seek out Manhattan hotspots.

Few tip Tony for his efforts. Tony doesn't seem to care. He really likes helping. And yes, laughing.

He knows me. And seemingly everyone at Fox. "Mister C.," he yells. "Your ties stink. But today's ain't so bad!" He jokes that his head is bigger than mine, and proves it by thrusting his cap atop my noggin. Gosh, if he isn't right! That's a big cap!

Like Tony, who's a big man. Maybe, by some people's standards, a simple man in a simple job. But I disagree. Anyone who can make normally blasé New Yorkers burst out laughing ain't just a simple man doing a simple job. Tony's better than that. And I like to think he's better than the people who scoff past, often ignoring him.

He is too decent to return their rudeness. Not now—this being New York at the holidays and all. Even the cynical sport a smile in this city this time of year. The difference with Tony is that he's been this way throughout the year. All but saying with his face what he feels in his heart: "Smile, world! It ain't gonna kill ya."

# The Preacher and His Wife

*November 15, 2004*

Sometimes you don't have to look far for heroes. Sometimes, they're right in front of you.

A Texas foster family comes to mind. He's a minister, she a minister's wife. Both love kids. All types of kids from all types of situations. Sometimes bad situations. Sometimes very bad situations. The minister and his wife are just a stop along the way for these kids. But what a stop. They can't control what happens to these kids' lives. But while those kids are with them, they try to give some meaning, some happiness, some purpose to those lives. And they do.

What they lack in a lot of material goods, they more than make up for in just *doing* good. They laugh with the kids. Play with the kids. Provide hope for the kids. Then they send them on their way, to new families, to finish their good work.

They get no press. No media mentions. But the minister's wife tells me their joy comes from a smile, and a connection. And a life touched.

I live a life talking to great leaders—CEOs, senators, and presidents. Leave it to a minister and his wife to remind me others can claim greatness too . . . without the title, without the money, without the status. But with something far richer . . . something called a heart.


## Have Anger, Will Soar

*September 8, 1999*

What do you think is the one big no-no in climbing the corporate ladder? The single most assured career killer? The thing that can prevent you from ever getting to that corner office— dare I say, any office?

It's not an education. It's not who you know, or who you don't know. It's not even your social skills . . . though this can affect those skills. No, I can sum it up in one word. The one thing that can decide whether you're a champ or a chump in business, and maybe in life in general, is anger.

You heard me right: Anger. It's not just a career killer, it's a killer, period. According to researchers at Duke University Medical Center, people who blow their top tend to blow off this planet early.

A page-one story in today's *Investors Business Daily* spells out the startling fallout. The personality traits of some law and medical students were charted over a twenty-five-year period. It seems the calmer personalities were outliving the angrier ones. Get this: Among calm lawyers, only 4 percent died by age fifty. Among the hostile ones, 20 percent died by fifty.

No one knows quite why this happens. Angry men, for example, are more likely to smoke and drink. But there's more. Temper tantrums can actually clog the arteries. And make you pretty miserable.

The upshot is this: Quit being so down.

Easy for me to say, since I'm so easily annoyed by so many things. Like that guy cutting me off in traffic. *Forget about it,* say the doctors. *Try to think of that fellow as a father rushing to get home to an impatient family. And that annoying, bullying boss as a guy who's just under a lot of pressure.*

And here's the kicker: If not for the sake of your health, then try it for the sake of your job. Upbeat, positive people get the raise and the promotion. Angry people sit and stew and carp, and soon they're being avoided. Before, ultimately, they die. Pfft. Just like that. And a lot sooner than the happy people who apparently drove 'em crazy. Go figure.

## Thank You, Becky. And Merry Christmas

*December 23, 2003*

The line at the cash register stretched around two clothing racks and at least three sales bins. People were getting restless. I was getting agitated. Why did I wait so long to do my Christmas shopping? And why on a Saturday, no less?!

I only had a few items. The person in front of me appeared to have bought out the entire store. We were all grumpy, all agitated, all very un-Yule-like, and all wanting to be anywhere but in this line, on this day, during this season.

Through my hissing and sulking, I distinctly heard someone laughing—make that guffawing. No, make that joking and kidding. It wasn't anyone in the line; it was the cashier waiting on that line. The woman at the register was in a positively wonderful mood. For the life of me, I couldn't fathom her good cheer. Every customer seemed grumpy. She was practically giddy. We were all stewing. She was sparkling.

"Well, how are you this fine day?" She belted out to the older man who sauntered up to her register. "Get all your shopping done today?" she asked.

He grunted something. I couldn't hear. She commented on his items: "Beautiful, just beautiful! You have wonderful taste."

He managed a smile, or was it a smirk?

"Boy, oh boy," she added, "I wish I was married to you!"

He definitely smiled this time. I distinctly heard him say something like, "Well, I hope she likes it."

"Oh, she will," she said. "You're such a nice guy! She'll be so thrilled Christmas morning!"

By now, he was positively smitten—delighted, in fact. He started joking with her. It was a remarkable transformation, from bummed to beaming in little more than a few minutes. And all because of this deliriously delighted woman behind the register. I still couldn't make her out. I was too busy trying to figure her out, and how the heck she could be in such a good mood when everyone she encountered was not.

She melted them all, one by one, scrooge by scrooge. As the long line wound its way closer to her, I finally made out her nametag. "Becky" was all it said. She seemed to be in her mid-fifties or so. Heavyset, with a great smile and big blue eyes . . . really big blue eyes. And a laugh—what a laugh! She kidded and joked, poked and teased. I wondered how and why those closer to the register seemed to be in a much better mood than those much further from the register.

I could see now the Becky effect. She was de-icing them, and re-nicing them. She was infusing them with the holiday spirit they no doubt had with them when they left their homes, but forgot after a while when the long lines and big crowds of holiday shopping started them longing to return to their homes.

Becky was amazing. She was fast and efficient, but personal and courteous at the same time. I could clearly see that she was moving as quickly as she could. There were a lot of people, but Becky had a lot of patience, and a lot of heart, and a lot of cheer.

By the time I got up to the register, she blew me away with her first line. Spotting the weekend stubble on my face, she wondered aloud, "Did you grow that while waiting on line?" I laughed out loud, and so did the couple in back of me.

Becky sorted through my items and discovered that one of them didn't have a price tag. I cringed. "Oh, I know this one," she said. "I think you got the last one, you devil. I hope she likes it."

"I hope so too," I said.

She pointed out that one of my items was dirty. "Probably fell on the floor," she said, and dashed over to the rack to get a cleaner, better one. Then, just as fast, she was back at the register—back smiling, back laughing, and back offering the very best for my family and me.

Then I was done, and Becky was on to her next customer, still sparkling, still kidding, still being all I should have been this holiday season.

Here was a woman deluged by the very worst the holidays could throw at her: grumpy people in a grumpy line that seemed to know no grumpy end.

But Becky didn't care. Actually, Becky did care. And that made all the difference to a clueless shopper who started on a line assuming the worst about the Christmas season, only to discover the very best of the Christmas season. Santa didn't do that. Fancy gifts didn't do that. Other people in that line didn't do that. Becky did that.

I wish I knew her last name, because I'd love to offer her, most of all, the merriest of Christmases, and the best of good cheer.

## What's Wrong with Having a Temper?

*January 13, 2004*

So Howard Dean has a temper. I wouldn't know, even though I've been closely following the guy. But apparently many of his Democratic opponents are making a big deal over it.

Frankly, I don't see what all the fuss is about. I mean, is a temper really a bad thing?

Look, I'm half-Italian and half-Irish. I figure I was born with a temper. My Irish mother used to joke about letting her more "cerebral" side prevail. Often, it didn't. But that's not my point here; this fuss about Dean's temper is.

I think we need more people with tempers. Tempers are good. Tempers show passion. Tempers show commitment to a cause and a determination to go after those who will block your cause.

Now, I don't mean that I'm in favor of letting anger take over your life. There's everything wrong with getting angry for nothing. But there's nothing wrong with getting angry for something.

Believe me, I am far from square on Dean's political positions. Some, like rescinding the president's tax cuts, are out-to-lunch. His view on the Iraq war, to me at least, seems naïve. But I do admire the guy for passionately believing these things, or at least looking like he passionately believes these things, apparently with a lot of emotion.

Opponents love to capitalize on a guy with a temper because they think they know how to push his buttons, or get him to snap. I know I sound crazy here, but I love it when candidates snap—when they show what really gets their goat.

I know it was a small thing, but remember when the first President Bush made a big stink about how he hated broccoli? I loved it! It was the first time I'd seen this guy get really passionate about something.

The same with Ronald Reagan, some years earlier when he was campaigning for the presidency. He made a big stink about who could and couldn't talk at a New Hampshire Republican debate, funded in part by the candidates themselves. "I'm paying for this microphone!" he shouted, and the rest was history.

I also remember the story of Bill Clinton losing it with economic advisers in the first few weeks of his administration, when, in an effort to appease the financial markets, his aides were calling for strict deficit-control measures. "I guess we're all Eisenhower Republicans," he allegedly snapped.

Lyndon Johnson used to throw things at television images of Walter Cronkite. Jack Kennedy went apoplectic when reluctant Southern governors weren't toeing his nonsegregation line. And who can forget how Harry Truman ripped into someone reviewing his daughter's singing abilities? When he was done with the guy, Truman vowed, the guy might need some support "down below."

These very human, in-your-face confrontations don't make me think less of these guys. They make me think more of them.

Sometimes candidates and politicians are so packaged, so restrained, so vanilla, that you don't get any real sense that they have any real concern for the people they're supposed to be fighting for. Showing a temper, maybe even throwing in a curse word or two, conveys passion, emotion, anger—all real emotions in an often very illusory world. I say, shout it, curse it, throw it, and have at it. We could all do a lot worse than to see the guys who want to be our leaders get a lot more passionate.

# Fast Markets

### August 26, 1997

What if the Dow crashed and no one was there to see it?

A little extreme, but it's pretty much the way I felt the Friday before last, when stocks were stumbling, and I was vacationing.

I mean, here I was at a quiet lakeside retreat, tucked deep in the woods in upstate New York. No television, but lots of lakes. No hot trading tips, but plenty of hot hiking trails.

Yet there I was routinely checking in on things via a phone line and the Internet, only to discover around 3:30 P.M. Eastern that the Dow was in freefall.

I felt obligated to tell someone about it at a country grocery just after the market closed.

"Hey, did you hear the Dow dropped nearly 250 points?" I blurted it out to almost anybody.

"No, didn't hear that," replied one local.

"Yeah," I said, "second biggest point drop ever."

"That so?" the guy responded.

"Guess some folks lost some money today," he added.

"Yea, a lot of folks," I chirped.

"Incredible," he said. "But not as incredible as it raining tomorrow on our peach festival. Might have to cancel the fishing contest and all."

Suddenly it occurred to me. To this guy, on this day, at this time, in this place, Wall and Broad seemed far away. Good thing.

# *ACKNOWLEDGMENTS*

I thought doing a second book would be easier, and that my reliance on many trusted colleagues and advisers would be less. I thought wrong! Just like I thought wrong that undertaking another book would be less of a hassle for my family. I don't think my wonderful wife and soul mate of a quarter century, Mary, would agree. She not only seamlessly kept our ship at home afloat, but also made sure our wonderful kids, Tara, Jeremy, and Bradley, were running along fine as well. My thanks to all of them. They are my bedrock. They are my life.

Increasingly a part of my life is a young man who opens me up to other views on life. Diego Romero bears special mention. He came into our family as an exchange student. Now we freely exchange ideas, including many picked up in this book.

To my wonderful sister and her husband, Arlene and Richard Krauter, my brother, Ron Cavuto, and my nephew, Shawn Phillips, and his wife, Melissa, special thanks as well. They always keep me close, and they always, always, keep me humble. For that, I'm eternally grateful! So, too, am I indebted to my wife's family, now *my* family—Anne Fulling for her heart, Frank and Mary Ellen Fulling for their decency, and Robert and Julie Fulling for their goodness.

My boss Roger Ailes and his fantastic wife, Beth, keep me grateful, too. They are dear friends who've stood by me in wonderful and challenging times alike. I wouldn't be where I am today without them, or have made half the insights included in this book without learning from them.

At work, I've learned that great programming comes from minds far greater than my own. My thanks to my editorial shepherds, Gary Schreier and Gresham Striegel, as well as Pamela Ritter, Sam Sayegh, John Huber, Andrew White, Alison Moore, Amanda Gershkowitz, William Gregson, Jennifer Altheide, David Asman, Brenda Buttner, Susannah Jabbour, Terry Keenan, Jodi Kirschner, Dagen McDowell, Michele Nunes, Jason Rosenberg, Tia Tiryaki, Stuart Varney, and so many other colleagues at Fox, for sticking to a credo we all hold dearly: better to be real and right, than fast and loose. And special thanks to my buddy, Hilda LaPolla, for making sure I at least try to *look* good, and to my always-there assistant, Anita Garay, for making darn sure I *do* good! I'd be lost without either of them! I wouldn't even know the time without Anita! Special thanks as well to my online pals who helped so much with my last book—Bert Solivan, Jason Ehrich, Andrea Bell, and Matt Court.

And what can I say about Judith Regan—a publisher who has a knack for seeing the story behind the title and the everyday drama in something else called life. Judith challenged me to think outside the box. Little did she know that I, like her, *live* outside the box! Or of her colleague and perhaps the best editor in the business, my guiding literary light, Calvert Morgan—always there, always reassuring, always challenging, and always improving. As were Paul Crichton, Heidi Krupp, and Laura Robinson in getting this book out!

Of course, none of this would be possible without my friend and career guru of more than a decade now—the ultimate lawyer's lawyer, Robert Barnett. He has kept me true to my writings, and better yet, truer to myself.

To Rupert Murdoch for trusting my instincts and proving you can be really rich and really decent at the same time! And to my dear friend Sean Hannity for always sticking up for me—and, in addition, for helping to make my last book a bestseller! And to the inimitable Duane Ward, who kept it a bestseller. And kept me on my toes!

So many people did so much to keep me so on target, including my friend, Angel Baez. There are many others too numerous to mention, but never, ever too numerous to forget. I am grateful for your guidance in my life. I am much more grateful that you all have been a part of my life.

# INDEX